NAVIGATING YOUR LANDSCAPE:

Finding Your Path Using A Moral Compass

BRENDA D. NEWBERRY

DEDICATION

To the navigators in my life: Maurice, my life partner and a man comfortable enough with his manhood to often be the only male accompanying spouse. We are looking forward to being healthy and celebrating fifty years of marriage in 2022. Also to Yasmin and Cherie, our patient, understanding and supportive daughters; my parents, maternal grandmother, and the generations past who provided the lessons on navigating our landscape; the current generation, who, I pray understand enough history to provide solid direction which creates gentle trade winds for the next generation as they navigate through life; and to the future generations—may you receive the maps to allow you to navigate the landscape for your life travels in this world and beyond.

TABLE OF CONTENTS

FOREWORD

It could not happen! Not in this life for sure! That is what one might predict if asked the chances for success, happiness, and fulfillment of the young lady who is the subject of this life story if told of the obstacles in her way as she pursued her goals, her dreams. In this remarkable and very personal memoir, Brenda Newberry recites where she came from and the struggles she had on her way to a multitude of achievements topped by her loving family. It is the story of a woman of great faith whose high level of achievement is startling in view of the challenges she encountered. It is a life story that should be read by young aspiring individuals and read more than once by young African American women who may be searching for guideposts as they launch their careers. It is a life story that awakens the reader to the axiom that success and fulfillment can be achieved given certain necessary attributes and disciplines.

In these pages Brenda looks back at where she came from and what contributed to her remarkable life. Of note is the close relationship she forged with her maternal grandmother, a strong willed, tough, deeply religious woman whose first marriage was to a sharecropper thirty-five years her senior. Brenda remembers that she could "curse like a sailor." Her family loyalty was joined with her intolerance for those on welfare. She made her living cleaning houses and offices after moving from the South to Gary, Indiana seeking more opportunity. Her high standards and discipline without doubt had an indelible impact on her granddaughter that could never be erased.

Growing up in the 1950s and 60s was challenging (to say the least) for a young African American female. Brenda learned early on from her parents and grandmother how important it was to get a good education. She knew that no one in her family had yet to attain a college education. She also came to realize that being black put her on the wrong side of a segregated society. She came to understand that most hotels and restaurants were not open to blacks nor restrooms in gas stations. Moreover, opportunities in the business world were limited not only because of her race but also her gender. It didn't stop there. She was to encounter rejection as well based on the issue of credit and whether or not the business was the right size.

With these innumerable obstacles it's hard to contemplate a life that would culminate in significant financial success and important honors. It is hard to grasp that at the peak of her career as she reached a point that she could deservedly rest on her laurels, she encountered a serious challenge to her health that might as well have ended her storied life. Once again she rallied her physical, emotional, and mental resources and triumphed over this foe as she had done so often in her earlier life.

This is truly an inspiring life story. The reader could justifiably ask how could it be done and what ingredients might combine to produce such a life story.

We learn from these pages that there were many people, factors, and circumstances which contributed to Brenda's history. First was Maurice, her constant, strong, and supportive partner who became the love of her life from a relationship that started in high school. Ever faithful, a man of strong character who shared the values that Brenda cherished. Talented and devoted, Maurice was the partner who strengthened and supported her through so many of the down drafts that occurred in her life. Aside from her grandmother, one must credit her parents and her two daughters who brought joy and vitality to her life.

In addition one learns from these pages the values and qualities of character that motivated and sustained her through all her travails and victories. Her commitment to education prevailed through her lifetime. Hard work and perseverance were deeply embedded in her. In addition, her inevitable and consistent focus on goals was a strong contributor to her success.

Perhaps most of all was her life-long faith and her firm conviction that her life was in the hands of her Creator. Her deep belief that there is a heavenly God who had a plan for her life never left her and was always a source of her enduring strength.

This inspiring life story is one that should be read and absorbed by all who may have come to believe that opportunity today is limited to those who are born with financial resources and connections. These pages establish that such is not the case.

-George Herbert Walker III
U.S. Ambassador to Hungary, 2003-2006

ACKNOWLEDGMENTS

I wish to thank those that requested that I write this book. Without your requests and encouragement, I would have never set sail on this journey to write.

I must thank God, not only for my parents and my life, but also for my experience with tongue cancer because for a time, it was not a given I would ever be able to speak again. So being unable to talk for a while made me realize it was time to write. Thankfully, I am now not only able to write but I can speak. I am grateful to be able to eat, swallow, taste, and enjoy cooking. Believe me, you should not take any of these simple things for granted.

I thank our neighbor, Dr. Lisa Ring, who immediately directed me to the right specialist after only one look at my mouth. Of course, I thank Dr. James Boyd, Dr. Robert Frazier, and Dr. Hsiao-Ou Hu, the medical team that assisted in my treatment and recovery. Because of them I am here to write this book.

I thank Maurice who has actually saved my life several times and continued to remind me to take time to write. His near-sighted orientation to detail was and continues to be a great accompaniment to my far-sighted global orientation. I looked out and saw the distant possibilities and he worked on the "how"—encouraging us to prepare to navigate later excursions. Because of him our possibilities and goals became our realities.

Our daughters deserve a thank you because we were weird parents that refused to use the map given by society, but navigated through less traveled territories marked by rough waters and "keep out" signs taking them right along with us. I thank them both for becoming the wonderful young women and mothers they have become, and I thank their spouses for climbing aboard for their journeys. I thank my grandchildren. They were also motivators for me to write so they might be encouraged and not become victims of difficulties but victors of opportunity. I pray they can set sail on their journey following the moral maps, for which the directions have withstood the test of time, through the strength and knowledge of the journey of their ancestors.

A huge thank you to Ambassador Walker, who did not hesitate to agree to write the foreword for this book. We worked together on various boards and as Air Force veterans, we both share a special affinity towards service, the love of this land of opportunity, and the belief of personal accountability teamed with a mutual respect for each other.

I want to thank Dr. Larry Keefauver and Pamela McLaughlin, my editors, and the staff at Xulon Press for their great assistance in this project.

Lastly, I wish to thank those that were steering ships along the way, helping me navigate and offering their prayers, assistance, opportunity, and support in various ways. Out of respect for your privacy, trying to keep the book a reasonable length, the fact that there were far too many of you to name, and the concern that I would accidentally miss some of you, I do not print your names. Many of you will recognize yourselves in this book and others will reflect and know they were a part of the journey. To all of you, I want to let you know that you did help, you made a difference, I remember, I appreciate, and I thank you!

PREFACE

So She Writes...

At the relatively young age of fifty-eight, I had surgery for squamous cell carcinoma on the right side of my tongue—tongue cancer. I half expected to have to deal with colon cancer because both my father and his father passed of that horrible condition. Even breast cancer would not have been a great surprise because of the statistics for women, but tongue cancer? After over 30 years of healthy living, a non-smoker, moderate alcohol use, married forty years with no HPV related strains, running or walking five to ten miles four to six days a week plus work with weights for muscle retention, I was totally surprised by this physical attack.

Reflecting on the weeks immediately after surgery, I clearly remember the burns on my neck and in my mouth from the radiation. I could not talk well and subsisted on a liquid diet of commercial protein drinks which all tasted like metal. I forced the drinks down because I did not want a feeding tube ever again! My energy levels were very low. The chemo process was horrible. The scars are physical, but the emotional scars were worse.

The day following the surgery, I was in shock at the extent of the invasion of my body to include the fact that I could not talk. A hemiglossectomy (a partial removal of the tongue), a neck dissection to remove twenty-three lymph nodes, a skin graft from my right forearm to reconstruct my tongue, and a skin graft from my left thigh to replace the skin taken from the right forearm were not quite bionic, but definitely shocking!

A tracheotomy, feeding tube, soft cast on my left arm complete with drainage tubes, a blood patch on my right thigh, severe scars on my neck complete with staples, and drainage tubes as well as IVs, and nursing care every two hours or less caused me to ask, "Why me? How could I possibly need surgery to remove cancer from my tongue?" I could not even talk at the time and it was not a given that I would be able to speak well ever again. Then it hit me.

God said, "Write the darn book!"

Though not implying I am a Moses or a Job type of person, I do have a great faith in God. I believe He does communicate with us and He does not allow us to miss His message or path. He often puts us on the path via correction or allows events and conditions to do so. By the same token I do not believe God punishes us, but He does allow consequences for our actions. However, in my mind I felt I had done nothing to result in these consequences. Faith tells me everything is for God's glory so challenges often are methods the Lord uses for a change of direction, a new path, modified journey or mission that ultimately glorifies Him.

Like a lump of clay in the hands of the Creator,
we are forever being molded by life's experiences.
– Feyisara Aladese

Public speaking was indefinitely delayed, and I perceived that God wanted me to stop talking and write. For over five years, associates would say at least every other month that I should write a book about how my husband and I had built a "successful" business from scratch with notoriety within the community and a solid cash flow with revenues hitting right around $20 million a year in "only" twelve years. After all, learning from the mistakes of others is much better than making your own.

We transitioned the company to employee-owned after twelve years, and at age fifty-five I was serving as a Director for two public companies, basically retired, and financially sound. Well, like most entrepreneurs, I was busy constantly. I never could find the time to actually sit down and put some thoughts on paper. Besides, what would it be about? What would be the title? Who would even read it? What would be the message? Then tongue cancer hit with a vengeance, so I submitted and began to write.

Do not worry this book is not about the cancer from this point forward, although I will definitely make some references to it here and there. This book is about *real* life, and how it is possible to execute towards your dreams. As an African American, regular person without influential contacts, famous parents or celebrity connections, how did I accomplish my dreams and goals? What did I learn? How can you, the reader, take away some practical wisdom and tips for fulfilling your dreams?

> **It is important that one not allow others to define them, their possibilities or their trajectory. One can choose to rise above the expectations and flee from those that would make them a victim or even cause them to feel like a victim.**

This book shares our experiences, stories, and life lessons. You will see some of what others have written about me or us from various sources. You will see how we learned from our experiences and walked through triumphs and some tragedies. Come, journey with us and discover some nuggets for living fully and successfully.

And so she writes...

First Again: *Life together in Air Force has Scott couple flying high* (Metro-East Journal September 14, 1978, by Jean Ann Bailey)

"We weighed the benefits as to what might go wrong and decided the service would enable us to travel, go to school, and save money at the same time."

– Brenda Newberry

INTRODUCTION

The Promise

Whatever a man promises to God or others, whether a vow or a
binding oath with a pledge, he must do. He is bound by his word:
no excuses and no exceptions. — Moses[1]

Maurice and I met in high school. I was fourteen and he was sixteen. We dated off and on until his senior year when we dated exclusively. My parents guarded me closely, and as with most parents, did not really like "the boyfriend." One time we were late from a date and my father met us at the car stating that Maurice was "less than a man."

Another time, Maurice was at our home visiting on a Saturday night. Of course with my parents at home. It was after 10:00 p.m. and past the time my parents insisted any company would have to leave. When Maurice's ride home was late, my father actually told him he would have to leave and wait outside for his ride home or walk. Maurice left and waited outside in the cold. My father was very strict! I also remember the time that we were sitting on the couch in the living room and my father was

---

[1] See Deuteronomy 30:2 VOICE

peeping through the outside window to keep an eye on us not realizing that we could see him. You can imagine my embarrassment!

When these things and other equally difficult parent challenges did not deter Maurice, my dad realized that it was very serious, but never backed off until after we had been married for several years.

Maurice went to Purdue University to study industrial engineering while I was a senior in high school. We wrote letters often and he would get his father to bring him back many weekends. One particular weekend was homecoming weekend. I did not win as the Homecoming Queen, but I was a candidate and had to select an escort as Maurice was not scheduled to be home that weekend. As the cars went on the field, I looked out and there he was! It was a great surprise and indication of his caring attitude to travel the distance just to be there with me for a special moment.

The next year, I went to Purdue majoring in biology with a goal to become a medical technologist. At first Maurice was a bit distant and I now know his reason was to give me space to decide what I wanted. This was because many of the "older" young men seek out freshmen girls. I had my share of interest, but my heart was with Maurice. At the end of that year, Maurice asked me to marry him.

We each called our parents to school and when they arrived we could see their nervousness. When we expressed our love for each other and desire to marry during the summer, they breathed a sigh of collective relief. Apparently, they were concerned that I might be pregnant so they were relieved that we wanted to get married. We received their consent and prepared to begin a life together. The one condition I had to make was to promise my grandmother to complete college because I would be the first generation in our family to do so, Maurice, too.

We were in love, we had our parents' consent, and we were determined to fulfill that promise. There was just one hitch, we were unable to retain financial aid for student married housing unless our parents did not claim us for taxes, so only our income or lack thereof was considered. We did not want to financially impact our parents, so we left campus and transferred to the Calumet Campus of Purdue. That meant working during the day and going to school evenings. Maurice got a job in the steel mill working in the coke plant. I first worked in a retail department store at which I was on their teen board in high school, then worked in a church-owned candy store after the department store laid me off. (The teen board was a group of teens from various high schools that provided the store with fashion advice, assisted with fashion shows, and helped with community outreach. The store also provided part-time jobs for the teens that were on the board.)

The rigor of work and school was tough for newlyweds because we did not have the same days off, school was a challenge, we made little money, and the coke plant of the steel mill was so dirty Maurice could not get the dirt off his eyes and fingernails. I shuddered to think what it was doing to his lungs even with using the issued equipment. We continued this from August through May. Then one day off, Maurice came to pick me up at the candy store and announced that he was strongly drawn toward joining the Air Force. His reason was for job training, the opportunity to complete his education for little to no cost, and travel. He had talked extensively with the recruiter. I immediately expressed my desire to join so I could complete my education, too.

After all, I had promised grandmother!

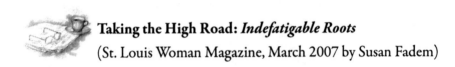 Taking the High Road: *Indefatigable Roots*
(St. Louis Woman Magazine, March 2007 by Susan Fadem)

"The frame of reference (in the 1960's and 70's) was, 'Go to college, get a good job, and stay there until you retire."
– Brenda Newberry

Chapter 1

SURVIVE AND THRIVE

Don't you remember the rule we had when we lived with you? "If you don't work, you don't eat." No excuses, no arguments—earn [your] own keep. Friends, don't slack off in doing your duty. – Apostle Paul[2]

Knowledge is power, information is liberating. Education is the premise of progress in every society, in every family.

– Kofi Annan

I n the early 1950s when I was born, the United States was hostile to Blacks, but it was and still is a land of opportunity if one works hard enough or harder than the rest. Far too many people are not willing to do what is necessary to achieve their goals, dreams or acquire what they envy of others. I was born to two very brown parents

My parents held the strong belief that education was the key because if one could read, they could learn and if one could learn, then the sky was the limit for opportunity to move up socially.

---

2 See 2 Thessalonians 3:10 MSG

and my maternal grandmother was extremely dark. My father looked American Indian and my mother was a gorgeous cafe au lait with very dark brown soft hair. I was, however, very "white looking" with nappy hair that had golden blond streaks, strange greenish brown eyes, and extremely skinny.

Maternal Grandmother

My maternal grandmother was tall, thin, and very black with very short hair, and had a harsh yet graceful demeanor. I remember her reading the Bible, smoking cigarettes, and listening to the gospel on the radio. She could also curse like a sailor. She took no bull from anyone as she protected her family in the best way she knew. My grandmother was proud and felt it a disgrace to be on welfare. She was rather a trailblazer and independently moved to Gary, Indiana for opportunity outside of life in the south where she was destined to marry another old sharecropper when her first husband died. Her first husband was thirty-five years her senior.

In Gary, she worked very hard cleaning houses and offices as the job market allowed. My mother, aunt, and uncles were raised very strict. They were expected to cook and clean as well as attend school and complete homework. My mother and aunt wore saddle oxfords which they polished and shined so well that people thought the shoes were new. They often told me stories of how others also thought they constantly had new clothes because grandmother made them wash everything and then iron the clothing extremely well.

In those days, my grandmother had the support of neighbors who would keep a watchful eye on the children. The neighbors not only watched, but were able to discipline in ways that would not necessarily be approved of today such as light spankings when children were young. As they got older, neighbors would send misbehaving children home from playing. The neighbors also had the option of telling grandmother if they misbehaved, in which case, they were often disciplined twice.

As a result, all four of those children graduated from high school which was an accomplishment for colored families with a female head of household. Grandmother finally met and married her second husband which resulted in a fifth child who was senior to me by only four years. When that husband passed from a steel mill accident, she was able to live on his pension/social security so she became a stay-at-home mom to my uncle, the only child left at home by then.

She took care of me often while my mother worked, and I played with my uncle and cousin who lived with my grandmother. They toughened me up a bit. I became somewhat of a fearless tomboy, but was too skinny to fully embrace it.

Early on, my grandmother would throw me on her hip and we were off wherever she needed to go. We were a unique pair with her being so dark and me so pale. In the fifties, people would question my grandmother when she carried me because they were not sure if she was the "Help" taking care of her charge or if I was her child. In retrospect, I simply looked mixed race but that was quite uncommon at the time. Sometimes if someone actually had the nerve to ask about us instead of just staring, she would tell them it was none of their damn business. Grandmother had no time for gossip or nosiness and was not intimidated by anything. I remember her as a strong woman that was independent and fiercely protective of her family.

I was oblivious to this issue of color and its impact until about the age of four. I was fortunate to live with a father and mother who did not discuss the mistreatment of Blacks in America in front of their children. They simply tried their best to live and create a decent home life. They held the strong belief that education was the key because if one could read, they could learn and if one could learn, then the sky was the limit for opportunity to move up socially. Grandmother, my parents, aunt, and uncles stressed the importance of learning and insisted we speak English properly and well.

Young Brenda at Christmas

Not So Blended

My father was previously married and had four other children; three girls and one boy. I never knew my step-siblings because in those days blended families were not a practice. Grandmother also did not like the fact that Dad was seven years older than my mom. My mother was pregnant before they married. I was born only four months after they were married. Rumor has it that I was only a few months younger than my step-brother from the previous marriage.

Brenda's Mother and Father

I later learned that Grandmother threatened that if I was born of a darker skin, she would be sure to tell Dad that I was not his. I was indeed my Dad's child. He looked more American Indian and had a grandmother that was named "Queen" and looked very white. (Those with any knowledge know that Queen was the name given to the "master's slave" or the master's offspring or favorite slave. Hence the legacy of slavery seems to follow hundreds of years later up through even the present day.)

As I think about it, perhaps slavery itself forced or caused non-traditional family structure devoid of blending families because often the children were offspring of the master, and therefore, blending families was definitely not welcomed. The impact of those practices existed for so very long, so as society progressed the acceptance and active engagement of step-children into the "new" families was delayed for many until recent times.

Improved With Challenges

During the late 1950s and early '60s, I remember the segregation. When we traveled to visit relatives, which was mostly for funerals, we had to pack food like fried chicken and bread, and be prepared to drive straight through because blacks were not welcomed in restaurants or hotels in those days. I totally remember not being able to stop at rest stops or gas stations to use restrooms. We had to stop by the side of the road or highway to relieve ourselves.

On one of our trips to visit relatives in Mississippi, I was about four years old and allowed to go shopping with my mother and aunts. The trip to the store from the relative's house was rather long and when we had shopped for only a short time, I had to go to the bathroom. Since we were not familiar with the store because the relative did not go with us, my mother did not know where to find the colored bathroom. As she searched, it was not quick enough for a four year old and I went right there on the floor in the middle of the store. Everyone stared and commented with vile words about how much like animals we were. That is when I fully encountered the issue of prejudice in a way that stuck in my young mind.

In the 1950s and '60s, the average black person still had to work in servant type roles. Mom cleaned houses and grandmother watched over me. Dad was in construction. Much like I notice today, many in construction finished work at 3:00 or 4:00 p.m. only to meet at a local bar for a beer or two before heading home. Sometimes the weather would change and they were off very early due to rain or severe snowfall. This took its toll and over the years, Dad became an alcoholic. He changed when he drank and became very verbally abusive to Mom.

By the mid-sixties, after the Civil Rights Act was passed, mom was able to upgrade and began working at a grocery store mostly on the evening shift. Money was tight. Whether Dad worked or not, the same amount of child support was still due. I later learned that sometimes Dad drank the money away and did not pay the child support much to my mother's surprise and disappointment. Mom trusted and was extremely disappointed by this, but she never left him nor talked despairingly about him to me. I just watched and listened, and tried to be "low maintenance" so I would be one less thing to cause her worry or sadness.

Once I was older and not being watched by grandmother, Mom expected Dad to "watch" me when she was not home, but he was often home very late and very drunk. Much to his credit, however, he never bothered me, but I have to admit that I really stayed out of his way, too. At the age of ten, I began completing the dinners Mom had partially cooked, did homework, read, and watched TV. In the summers, I would relax, read, and spend time outside with my cousins who lived next door. One summer in junior high, I even taught myself to touch type on the typewriter and was able to type over sixty words per minute. I memorized the keys and become quite proficient. Little did I realize that many years later, the advent of the computer, PC, and beyond would make this skill personally and professionally very useful. This is one of many examples of "kisses from God" I have received through my life's journey.

Nuggets for Living Fully and Successfully

Our business and life mission statement included the phrase, "build careers and enhance lives." We personally demonstrate a strong work ethic and want to share all that we have learned with the readers of this book as well. Therefore, at the end of each chapter we will offer this interactive section to give you the tools to build your career and enhance your life so you can live fully and successfully. We have found that it is important to learn, but equally as important to actually take action. If one does not apply what they learn, then the learning is in vain.

Action without knowledge is dangerous, knowledge without action is useless.   – Walter Evert Myer

Below are some of the life concepts given in this chapter. Check off the ones you are already using and circle the ones you may need to begin to implement in your own life.

- It is important that you do not allow others to define you.
- It is important that you do not allow others to limit your possibilities or your trajectory.
- If you do not work, you do not eat.
- Do not slack off in doing your duty.
- Education is the key for opportunity.
- You can teach yourself or learn a skill that you can use later in life.
- If you work hard you can achieve success in life.

What It Takes: *How to Succeed Anyway* (St. Louis Small Business Monthly, August 2011, by Jeremy Nulik)

"Denying there are some issues does not help," Brenda says. "However, it does hurt to allow oneself to become a victim or paralyzed from challenges. After all, we are all working for something greater than ourselves and to not appreciate your blessings and do your very best is an insult to the greater good."

Chapter 2

BUILDING CHARACTER

You cannot dream yourself into a character; you must hammer and forge yourself one.   **-Henry David Thoreau**

During the early years, we were very poor. Though I was loved by family, the rest of the world treated me horribly. So much so, in fact, that I had to gain internal fortitude realizing that I had to love myself and work to take care of myself. This was not without the faith and knowledge of God. Because of my belief in God, I knew I was not totally alone. I knew I had the love of God.

My goal was not to be a burden to anyone—to be low-maintenance. This is something I still referenced as a business owner; calling "good" employees "low maintenance" or difficult employees "high maintenance."

What is "low maintenance?" In my mind it is being conscientious and self-motivated so any leader, boss or even my parents would consider me

> Over time I found that being "low maintenance" had a by-product of increased learning and creating a strong foundation of character.

a benefit rather than "difficult" or requiring constant attention. It was important to do my job, do it the best I could, researching, reading, and not requiring much attention. Rather than always needing something, I tried to accomplish the task or goal using the "tools" provided.

It has remained important for me to make the lives of others easier even if it impacted me physically, mentally or emotionally. Over time, I found that being "low maintenance" had a by-product of increased learning and creating a strong foundation of character. In fact, I realized it was actually a form of serving and rather biblical in that we would probably try to be "low maintenance" if we worked and lived directly for God.

Most of the day-to-day early childhood memories are a blur partly because there was little to no drama. I was expected to do my best without complaint, so I did. After all, low maintenance also meant little to no drama. Mom and Dad worked hard for our food, clothing, and shelter. They insisted that I do my best in school because education was the way out of poverty. They made sure I realized college was an expectation. Therefore, school was very serious business. Their belief was that one cannot miss work or school unless they were in the hospital or dead. That carried over into my own school and work life as well, and resulted in my personal desire to be reliable, consistent, and low maintenance.

Life was basically school, grandmother's house for visits, home, ballet and modern dance classes, swim lessons, Girl Scouts, and church. Ballet, dance, and swim lessons were all character building and kept me busy as well as out of trouble. These lessons and activities were costly, but my Mom was determined to build character, confidence, and ability in me. She worked extra hard and sacrificed to ensure she could pay for these lessons. My Mom realized that every skill, no matter how good or bad one was, provided lessons in character building.

Strengthening Character

Ballet lessons were fun; I thoroughly enjoyed them. I was not very good or the best in classes, but the music and having to learn specific steps was very enjoyable. However, it was what was then called modern dance that really caught my attention. It was free flowing and expressive. The owner of the dance studio was a wonderful teacher. I loved getting caught up in the music. When I was home alone, I would often just dance and dance, and continued dance lessons until I went to college. Little did I know this dance training was preparation for cheerleading in high school! God was at work in my life even at that young age!

Brenda Ballet Student

Mom and Dad also loved to go roller skating and bought me my first pair of roller skates at four years old. I still gleefully reflect on roller dancing with my Dad. He was smooth and because of dance lessons, we were smooth out on the skate floor together. We did moves like they did professionally with specific cadence going from front to back and moving our feet in perfect precision. It was great fun and I later used that experience to become a skate guard in college where I earned a few extra dollars.

My parents were also in a bowling league and taught me how to bowl quite young as well. Dad had this horrible looking hook ball where on the back swing he would turn his hand upside down. He and Mom were both great bowlers; I also became quite good at bowling.

I was and am amazed at what they were able to do with so little money. It was also amazing how those activities provided a foundation of skills, knowledge, and character. Becoming somewhat good or proficient at many things gives one a bit more courage to take on other challenges.

My parents always prayed and taught me about God, but we did not attend church frequently because my Mom had to work many weekends and nights. About sixth grade, I felt a call and began to attend a church down the street. It was Episcopalian. After a year or so, my parents wanted to attend church as well and we began attending a Baptist church that I continued attending until I married in that same church and joined the Air Force.

Other wonderful memories are from Girl Scout summer camps. The food, songs, campfires, and learning about nature were fabulous experiences for me. When I would come home with pictures of clouds and trees, my parents would ask where the pictures were with the other girls. In hindsight, I am not sure if the reason I had no friends at camp was because I was not outgoing and interested or because I was colored. (My nappy hair was a dead giveaway.) I was brought up as an only child and really was not interested in the other girls because I would hear them talking negatively about each other. I knew I was not exempt from that when I was not present, so I preferred to just keep to myself rather than participate in their gossip and two-faced behavior.

Learning to swim at camp was great, but I was not very good with combing out my nappy hair so I always returned home with a horrible, tangled mess. Because of Girl Scouts I was not afraid of water or nature. We had cabins when we were younger, but as we got older, we spent several days in tents and lived in the woods where we had to make our own "latrines" with trees and rope. It was so much fun! Little did I know it was in preparation for Air Force Basic training! Looking back I see God at work again, preparing me for what was to come!

In junior high, because of the Girl Scout swim lessons, my parents allowed me to enroll in life guard lessons with the YWCA. Another girl who was light-skinned as well as beautiful with straight wavy hair (what Blacks called "good hair") and I were the only Blacks in the class. However, my nappy hair was a challenge to prepare for school the very next day. But I took on the challenge and was up late those nights getting my hair in order for school.

Most Black females did not want to get their hair wet so they chose not to learn to actually swim. With the support and encouragement of my parents to not let others define what was possible, I was comfortable being different. Not only could I swim, I became a strong swimmer and felt I was strong enough to save lives because I had passed the lifeguard certification test! What a boost to my self-confidence!

The girl from my lifeguard class and I became good friends, later taking part in a local theater production of Kismet as dancers. This musical required many hours of after school practice. It was during this time that I met Maurice and we became girlfriend and boyfriend. Often Maurice and her boyfriend would come to practice. We would sneak in kissing between our practice of the routines. Most Blacks in our town did not even think about being part of a musical, but again it did not matter. I was determined not to let others determine what I could or could not at least try.

At sixteen, I was selected as a high school representative to a local department store which included a part-time job as part of their teen program. The program had a process and I made sure I did what was required to get the referrals I needed. Community involvement such as being in that Kismet production, as well as achieving good grades, and participating in extracurricular school activities are what got me the position, but others looked for reasons for my selection other than the hard work involved.

The gossip in high school was that I was selected because I looked white and white classmates felt it was because I was Black and the store needed Black representation. People can be so cruel, but I learned early on that denying that some issues existed did not help nor did allowing myself to become a victim or paralyzed by the challenges help either. There was a determination within me to be the best I could possibly be at whatever I tried to do even when it meant others disliked me. I was less concerned about what others thought because I knew, observed, and learned early on that young and old will or could dislike and talk negatively about you regardless of what you do whether good or bad. Therefore, I felt I might as well do "good" and be disliked for that rather than do "badly" and not only be disliked but also be in trouble and miserable.

Maurice turned out to be the love of my life. At first, like most boys, Maurice was rather a "player" and talked to and dated several girls. However, by his junior year, things became more solid and steady between us. We went to school dances together and by his senior year we were really close.

In high school I tried out for the cheerleading squad, busting my butt and learning no-hand flips using pillows on a hardwood floor at home. Though I had been blessed to have taken ballet and modern dance, I had no gymnastic experience so I had to basically teach myself to do those "no hand" flips and cartwheels in preparation for tryouts. Hard work paid off and I did make the cheering squad, but once again others tried to judge me. The white girls said I made it because I was Black. The Black girls said I made it was because I looked white. Maurice said I made it because as a captain in ROTC and member of the drill team he was one of the judges. No one knew or thought I worked very hard for it.

Brenda Cheerleading

No matter, I was not a victim. I knew I had worked hard, had the bruises to prove it, and made the cheerleading squad because of what I had put into it. That brought me great enjoyment. Women were not much into sports in those days, so cheerleading was a way to be somewhat athletic.

Education Is the Key to Independence

Maurice graduated from high school, was given the opportunity and gladly accepted the challenge of attending Purdue University. With about 1500 African Americans out of 20,000 students at the time, the university was not yet very racially diverse. However, quite a few people from our high school went there. After reviewing all the options and knowing Maurice and I really loved each other, I decided to attend Purdue as well. A combination of loans, grants, and scholarships as well as monthly payments by my parents provided the financial help I needed to attend. Maurice majored in industrial engineering. My major was biology as I planned to go into medical technology.

Maurice and I became very close during my first and his second year of college and basically realized we had a similar philosophy about life. We agreed right from the beginning how important it was to focus on our goals and achieve a good education. We studied together into the late hours and refused to participate in the constant card playing and partying that some other people did. So many students did not take the opportunity seriously. We did have fun and attended some parties. I roller skated and we did "hang" with some friends sometimes. However, we did not allow the friends to derail our concentration nor did we participate in their destructive behaviors.

Late in my freshman year, Maurice asked me to marry him and I said yes. He had already given me a promise ring in high school that my parents hated, so we were not sure about their reaction to our news.

When we called our parents to travel to the university to ask them to meet with us to tell them we wanted to marry, we expected them to be upset or try and talk us out of it. They did not. Suddenly we realized they had wondered what this meeting was all about and were so happy I was not pregnant that they peacefully agreed to our union.

Maurice was three months from turning twenty-one; I was two months from turning nineteen years old. We were married that August thinking we would just immediately return to Purdue. We had to transfer from the main campus so we could work to support ourselves and go to college. Financial aid was dependent on income and our applying on our own would have impacted our parent's taxes that year so we did not apply for or receive financial aid. We would have to wait until the next year, so we just transferred to the regional campus.

I had promised my grandmother that I would complete college and was determined to keep that promise. We both knew we had to accomplish that goal of graduating from college for ourselves and our family. They had all worked very hard as had the generations before them to earn us the right to an education. We could not and would not negate their sacrifices!

Maurice got a job in the steel mill, and I worked at a candy store for the church. We were working days and going to school in the evenings. It was not an easy life and one that, if continued, could have jeopardized completion of our education. The steel mill where Maurice worked was extremely dirty work and safety was always a concern, but the pay was decent. Maurice would come home with black around his eyes resembling mascara and hands that looked as if he has played with charcoal. The candy store did not pay very much at all, basically minimum wage. We lived with my parents for a short time until we had saved enough to move into an apartment.

Getting our first apartment was a challenging experience. One that reinforced my life view. It is important to honestly state your case with respect as well as possible with conviction and not give up. Do not become a victim and do not let others define you based on the actions of other people. As Blacks in America, people so very often tried to define us based on the horrible behaviors of others. But we were not horrible! We were good people that had good families! We had the funds and employment, but they did not want to rent to us because we had no credit history. Their experience was that given our youth and lack of a credit history, we would not consistently pay our rent and would create problems.

The major problem was no credit history. You know the "what comes first the chicken or the egg problem"? We finally said insistently, "If no one gives us a chance, we will never have a chance." The apartment complex director decided to give us a chance and rented to us with our parents co-signing in spite of us not having a credit history. We were disappointed that our parents had to co-sign, but glad we finally had a place of our own. Perseverance paid off, not settling for being a victim.

One day on a day off, Maurice stopped by the Air Force recruiting office while I was still at work at the candy store. He was convinced by the recruiter that he could work, gain a skill, finish his education, and travel. When he presented it to me, my first reaction was to tell him I was joining, too. After all, I had promised my grandmother that I would definitely finish college when we got married. This seemed like a way to guarantee that I would have a good job, acquire a skill, get my education, and travel, too. We joined at the same time and were the first couple from the region to enlist.

Brenda, Maurice, and Air Force Recruiter

It was the recruiter's "dream come true" as he got two enlistees at once. The recruiter even invited us to a party at his home to have his wife and friends tell us how good a life in the Air Force was for them.

Timing did not allow many choices for Air Force job classification categories, so both Maurice and I were slotted for base supply (647xx). We were enlisted and off to Texas in June after the college semester was over. It was the first airplane flight for both of us. Very rarely these days would one be over twenty years old when they first flew on an airplane. Of course, our parents did not to want us to leave and our friends thought we were nuts, but looking back it was a spectacular decision at the time for us. That was the start. We were off to see the world and what a great journey of experiences and learning it was going to be!

Next, let's explore the foundational principles so essential to character building.

Nuggets for Living Fully and Successfully

I firmly believe anybody can do what I have done if they just take advantage of opportunities and not seek shortcuts. Every life experience, whether good or bad, creates opportunities either in the short-term or long-term.

- *Watch for opportunities (Ephesians 5:15-17).*
- *When you see one, take advantage of it.*
- *Do not let anyone tell you that you cannot even try.*
- *Do not let anyone define who you are.*
- *Seek to excel at whatever you do (Colossians. 3:17).*
- *Work for and to please God not man (Colossians 3:23).*

Life together in Air Force has Scott couple flying high *(by Jean Ann Bailey Metro-East Journal Staff September 14, 1978)*

"The two became the first married team from the central recruiting area in Chicago to enlist in the Air Force. Both attended technical school at Lowry Technical Training Center in Denver, Colorado, to become supply specialists. The couple was then sent to Davis-Monthan Air Force Base in Tuscan-Arizona, and then to Torrejon."

Chapter 3

TWELVE FOUNDATIONAL PRINCIPLES

These twelve foundational keys can be applicable for success in life, career, and business; at least they were for me. You may have already seen some of them

> You sow in the wind, but you reap in the whirlwind—both good and bad.

in the chapters before this one and you will see them in future chapters. I do not point them out specifically because they are provided as a reference for thought and not as a twelve step program or twelve things to do for success. They explain some of the aspects of life that became clear as I reflect back over the years.

Before I give these twelve keys, I would like to point out that the most important philosophy Maurice and I have learned that we want to pass on to the next generation is that when one does good for others and the world, good will flow back to us in many ways. I often repeat a saying I heard from a church elder, "You sow in the wind, but you reap in the whirlwind—both good and bad." When a seed is sown or planted, the yield is great. For example, an apple seed will yield an entire apple tree yielding many more apples. Not just one. When flowers, grains or trees blossom, the wind blows those seeds far away. The point is to do good, but realize the world you live in has human frailties. Your blessings may not come from the fields you plant, but from faraway places and seemingly unconnected people.

#1–Be as independent as possible. No one can expect their parents to take care of them forever. So self-reliance is a given necessity. This also involves taking responsibility for one's life and decisions. In other words, do not blame anyone or anything else for one's personal decisions and the resulting consequences especially after the age of eighteen. Nothing or no one makes you feel, think or do anything. Yes, outside forces do influence your decisions including your past, your relationships, and your circumstances. But you and only you can make the decision to do or not do something. Independence's cousin is responsibility. Now do not get me wrong. I am not speaking of going it alone or not having faith in God. I am simply saying that it is important to think through decisions, pray, prepare, be willing to do the work, and then accept the outcomes.

#2- Set personal goals, work at them, and accomplish them. Most people will not be cheerleaders, but will help celebrate or recognize what is accomplished especially if they believe it will be beneficial to them. Some may assist in times of trouble, but often they are uncomfortable as if your trouble will rub off on them. I know the Christian and human comments and statements about being "there" for each other in times of trouble, but do not be surprised if you do not have as many friends as you thought.

People seem to love to hear about the troubles of others which may account for the current popularity of "reality TV" which concentrates on the dysfunctional situations of others. It appears that it makes them feel better about themselves. Personally, I was all about seeing what was possible and trying to accomplish it. I did not search for shortcuts nor did I search for other's problems to make me feel better about my own. As a

Black in America, I came to believe shortcuts were not for me, but also that very few goals are impossible if one is willing to "do the heavy lifting."

With God all things are possible, so create your goals and execute towards them. Look at what others have done to accomplish those things you wish to accomplish, and try to do those things that are possible within the paths that have been assigned to you. It may appear as if others had an easier road and perhaps they did, but that is generally the exception not the rule. Most work very hard to achieve "their success." Hard work and perseverance are what make the impossible possible. Remember, not to plan is to surrender the initiative or the proactivity to someone or something else.

#3–Remain humble yet focused. Do not let the attention you receive when you achieve inflate your ego. Remember, no one chooses their parents or where they are born. This keeps us humble because we know God is the reason for our existence and accomplishments. This helps keep the ego in check. Life can change drastically in the blink of an eye so we must not be smug when we find ourselves in some limelight or having achieved substantial goals. It is for God's glory and not ours lest we forget our humble beginnings.

Humility recognizes that I am limited and whatever accomplishments and achievements come my way require both my focus and hard work (faith without works is dead), and also, the participation and grace of others most particularly and first of all, God. I remember when going through cancer treatment I often thought about the fact that I never questioned "why me" when life went well, therefore, being challenged with cancer did not give me the right to question "why me" either. Since I knew God provides blessings, I had to also accept the fact that He allows challenges in our lives as well. Remaining humble during great times allows one to accept the challenging times with grace.

#4–Seek to add value to others while working towards your goals.
There is always a better way to do things. There is always a need to be met.
Every problem has a solution. "We make a living by what we get, but we
make a life by what we give" (author unknown). Find the solution to
someone else's problem and you are well on your way to being a success at
what you do. Their success contributes to your success. Service to others
opens the door of opportunity. Ultimately, we must learn to love and work
with others instead of
using others and working
just for or by ourselves.
Helping and enriching
the lives of others is important.

> **Believe and know that you are blessed with whatever it is, time, skills or material blessings, to be a blessing to others.**

#5–Chose Your Friends Wisely. Help them if possible and feel free
to say "no" if you cannot. Some people can be cruel, jealous, self-serving,
and self-absorbed so do not let them deflate your personal success either.
Do not be surprised or dismayed by the attitude of others. Just stay focused
on what you have set as your personal goals and do not give up! Remember
to do good, but realize the world you live in has human frailties. God will
be your cheerleader and bring the right people at the right time into your
life. Remember that we are not only judged by the company we keep, but
we are also influenced and often significantly impacted by that company.
As such, we need to develop relationships that raise the moral, ethical, and
performance bar for us instead of pulling us down.

#6–Your life is not about you. Life is not about me, myself, and I,
but what I contribute to others in various ways from social to emotional
to financial. "If you plant for days—plant flowers. If you plant for years—
plant trees. If you plant for eternity—plant ideas and ideals into the lives
of others" (S. Truett Cathy, founder of Chick-fil-A). Do no wrong to
others regardless what they do to you and you will reap your reward in

like kind. Do not get me wrong. God sees you as special. He loves you and seeks to redeem you. But you have a legacy as a servant, a teacher, and a leader to improve the lives of others. Selfishness says it is all about me. Servant leadership means that the one who serves first becomes the ultimate example or leader for others.

#7–Work hard and work as if for God. Do your very best in all situations and go above and beyond. "We never realize our greatest potential until we perform at our very best" (S. Truett Cathy, founder of Chick-fil-A). People are fickle. They love underdogs and yet they try to tear down those that do well. Accomplish what you will, but do not expect approval or acceptance from others along the way. In fact, expect just the opposite. Just remember, it was and is never about "them." It is about your journey with and for God. People can and will find ways to be negative towards those doing well, but ignore that and do well because it glorifies God.

#8–Eliminate negative people. Associate only with people you can be proud of whether they work with you or for you. Stay away from negative people and remember the less they know about you personally the fewer possibilities for jealousy and the less damage they could cause to you. Keep your eyes and focus on your God-given goals. Ignore the people around you that would rather see you suffer and may chide you for working so hard. I was often chided and asked why I worked so hard, as if my hard work hurt them. Let them laugh at your determination or "stupid hard work" and discipline. Quietly go about your business because sharing too much of your "good stuff" can breed jealously or distain. Be somewhat mysterious yet always be genuine. As I mentioned earlier, chose the right kind of friends and keep your distance from those who are evil, selfish, negative, critical, and just plain angry and bitter all the time. I often misjudged character, so do not beat yourself up if you accidentally allow yourself to be misled by someone you thought was good and positive yet turned out to be "bad news." Note the lesson and move on.

#9–Flee from a negative or draining environments. If one is making your world difficult, prepare to leave that place as soon as possible and leave them to wreak havoc where they may be "working." Retaliation is not an option, it is a distraction. If one is to stay focused and not be a victim, one does not need distractions. Always seek those places, people, and situations that challenge as well as nourish you. Positive people and places strengthen you; negative people and places drain you emotionally, mentally, physically, and spiritually. Sometimes you need to remain for various reasons but stay focused, do the right things, do your best, and pray for guidance about when and where to go. I cannot tell you how He will work in your life, but God will always have the path forward for you.

#10 – Do not whine. When challenged or disappointed, quickly get over it, and work with the cards that are dealt. Do your best with what you have, both the good and bad. Everyone has the mixture of good and bad areas of life whether it is a dysfunctional family or a difficult spouse. From the outside, it would appear that others have it better, yet many have it much worse. Either way, forget about it. Concentrate on your goals and the path God has for you and use it for good. Know the challenges as well as the good things ahead are for your personal growth if you just meet those challenges head on! If you find people are distancing themselves from you or avoiding your calls, emails, and social encounters, it could be because they are tired of your self-pity and whining!

#11–Use your talents. Do not waste your God-given gifts. Every skill you have is God-given. It is not appropriate to allow yourself to become a victim. Ask yourself how to best use your gifts and then go and use them. Strive to be challenged and then handle the challenge. Work so you are not needy. Be as strong, but also as kind and humble as possible. Continue to ask yourself if you are using the gifts of time, talents, and treasure God has provided or just wasting them. There may be people that prefer to look better by ensuring you are kept from using your talents. Refuse to be controlled in that way. Use your talents because that is why God blessed you with them.

#12 – Every decision counts. Decisions made at every age and stage in life may and probably will define where you find yourself in your future. Opportunities come and go based on past foundational preparation so keep working, preparing, and staying on the straight and narrow as much as possible. Camping out for a while or refusing to make a necessary decision could set you back for months, years or even decades. It is your journey and your decision. Accept and live with the consequences of your decisions. Remember, inaction is also making a decision. No matter how small a detail seems, those who are faithful in the details can be trusted with greater responsibility and prosperity. Every decision does count and makes a difference both in our lives and the lives of others.

These foundational concepts may seem indicative of a rather strange person, however, they do define how my results were accomplished by a complex, challenging yet difficult journey. These foundational attitudes were the very reason for achieving what many view as personal and business success. They required a lot of "outside the box" faithful thinking and actions. Following the crowd and what was expected was not a preferred option. In fact following those with admirable goals was very hard work, and I have found that the "crowds" generally did not follow them. Going above and beyond what most expected was important to achieving each goal. Most people spend time looking for shortcuts rather than doing the "heavy lifting," but I was determined to achieve even if it meant doing the heavy lifting was heavier than I thought.

Life is not perfect for anyone. Life can be totally unfair and often is for everyone. God nor man promises fairness. Wealth, intelligence, and even faith never insulates us from trials, tribulations, and suffering. Nothing guarantees fairness. What is important for getting the most out of life is how we respond to our circumstances.

Life's meaning, purpose, and ultimately experiencing comfort, peace, and joy will be determined by our choices and responses. It is all based on how we choose to look at life. When our view is through faith and guidance from God, life can be great and peaceful. We each get to choose! Now, we can move from these foundational keys into facing the challenges of life and work that we continuously encounter.

Nuggets for Living Fully and Successfully

Check off the ones you are already using and circle the ones you may need to begin to implement in your own life.

12 Foundational Keys
- #1–Be as independent as possible.
- #2- Set personal goals, work at them, and accomplish them.
- #3–Remain humble yet focused.
- #4–Seek to add value to others while working towards your goals.
- #5–Choose your friends very wisely.
- #6–Life is not about me, myself, and I, but what you contribute to others in various ways from social to emotional to financial. Are you contributing to others?
- #7–Work hard and work as if for God.

- #8–Eliminate negative people. Keep your interim achievements to yourself so others do not have an opportunity to derail or discourage you from the ultimate goals.

- #9–Flee from negative or draining environments. Always seek those places, people, and situations that challenge as well as nourish you.

- #10 – Do not whine. When challenged or disappointed, quickly get over it and work with the cards that you are dealt.

- #11–Use your talents. Do not waste your God given gifts. Continue to ask yourself if you are using the gifts of time, talents, and treasure God has provided or just wasting them.

- #12 – Every decision counts. Decisions made at every age and stage in life will probably define where you find yourself in your future. Remember, inaction is also making a decision. What decisions have you paralyzed with inaction?

For Brenda, the honors just keep rolling in... (*The Stars and Stripes*, by Mike Spear 1978)

Brenda won Air Force recognition when she was selected as one of twelve Outstanding Airmen of the Year in the Air Force for 1978. "It all happened so fast," she says. "It was hard to believe I would achieve it. I really do appreciate the support and encouragement I got in my duty sections."

Brenda Basic Training

Chapter 4

ACCEPTING THE CHALLENGES WHERE GOD LEADS

Anybody could do what I have done if they just take advantage of opportunities. – Brenda Newberry sharing during an interview with *Metro-East Journal Staff Reporter*, Jean Ann Bailey.

B asic training was in San Antonio, Texas. We were separated and Maurice was off to his squadron and I was off to mine. It was tough but also very much like Girl Scout camp for me. Maurice's letters gave me hints to make basic training "easier" and as a result, I became dorm chief. Maurice was a squad leader. Easier just meant working with the other women, identifying those with the best skills that were needed, and convincing them to work together letting those with the skills do the inspected tasks for everyone.

For instance, those that passed inspection with praise about their shoes for the shine would shine shoes for several girls. They in turn might be great at making the bed so they would make several beds. Others ironed exceptionally well so we formed an ironing group. I will not give details of the many other hints here because that might undermine the basic training program or spoil the experience for others. Bottom line, identifying the best skills within the team and "trading" services until everyone was "perfect" for our daily inspections resulted in team "perfection." The lessons in basic training taught us so many things about people, the country, organization, and self-discipline. It was life changing in a positive way and much of those skills and lessons are used and remain with us today.

Next we were assigned to technical training school in Denver, Colorado. Since we were married, we were able to live off base which provided companionship and the opportunity to focus and study together while growing in our love for one another. As a result of the focus, study and concentration, we graduated from technical training first and second in our class. It was amazing to us that it made the press back home and our parents were quite proud. We were only trying to do our best. The visibility was simply an unexpected bonus.

Brenda and Maurice in Uniform

Following technical training school, we were assigned together in Tucson, Arizona and worked in different areas of base supply, learning and enjoying ourselves as we grew in maturity and knowledge. It was a Strategic Air Command (SAC) base and it was obvious that the overall mission was important. Everything had to be done well and spit shine was real. We learned that concrete should shine and that white gloves were used even outside of basic training. Base supply was in a warehouse, but it was pristine in cleanliness and performance.

USAF Technical Training Full Class

Processes had to be followed or the pilot would be in an aircraft without the proper part or the mission could be delayed if we failed to do our jobs right. I drove forklifts, and yes they are as much fun as they appear, and I also drove ton and a half trucks. I worked the parts receiving line as well as the reject room for parts that were damaged. We learned that every task and job had a purpose and was important. Even clean and sanitary latrines were important. No job was too small or unimportant because directly or indirectly, every job was related to mission accomplishment.

After about nine months, we were asked if we would cross train to become drug abuse counselors. This was because we were a young, clean-cut couple and they wanted to modify their approach to begin counseling couples. In those days of the Vietnam War, it was reported that far too many younger service men and women were drug or alcohol dependent and were impacting their family unit. Of course, this could impact the Air Force mission as well. We jumped at the opportunity because we were sent to learn to become counselors and could leave the warehouse. While base supply was important work, we knew that counseling was even more critical and that work was interesting as well. We attended courses about marriage and relationships which were probably instrumental in own our long lasting marriage. One very important lesson was to totally eliminate the "d" word from our vocabulary. In other words, we were encouraged to agree that we would never threaten divorce at any time in our marriage no matter how heated the discussion or argument.

Every opportunity and challenge provides lessons even when least expected. As life would have it, though, this door was about to be closed while another door opened. I received orders for Torrejon, Spain! It was upsetting because it derailed the cross training we were involved in, and Maurice had not received his orders! We discovered that keeping couples together was not necessarily a priority in the military. We had to appeal to many people, but finally orders were cut for Maurice. After spending time at home with family, we flew off to Spain together in December. In less than two years in the Air Force, we were off to Spain!

Life in Spain

Initially, it was a great culture shock. No central heat or air conditioning in the places we could afford. It was cold, damp, and smelled different. Lukewarm showers was the norm. The food "on the economy" was different but good. Spain definitely was not the United States!

It turned out to be a great experience. We bought a Fiat Sports Spider convertible which we were able to sell three and a half years later for the same price we bought it. We traveled Spain and some parts of Europe. I even traveled to East and West Berlin before the wall was torn down.

Brenda and Fiat Sports Spider Convertible

While there, I learned to operate a Univac 1050 remote system, a keypunch machine, drove a fork lift, and a ton and a half truck. There was so much to learn and do. The computer work would later mean a career for me.

We also found time to go out to clubs with friends and attend the University of Maryland European Division. We not only completed our Bachelor degrees in Business Management from the University of Maryland European Division, but also our Master's degrees in Business from Webster University in St. Louis when we were reassigned there after our assignment ended in Spain (where I later became their first female non-lay, first African American, and first alumni Board of Trustees Chair). Our minors were psychology and human resources respectively.

I was also able to pursue my love of interpretive dance by teaching a creative dance class. We often toured as a dance troupe in many of the local Spanish communities. I found the Spaniards very receptive to our performances. It was the first time many of these communities had ever seen Black interpretive dance.

Interpretive Dance Troupe

We both learned so much during this time in our lives and it provided a foundation of being "low maintenance" as well as God and self-directed.

"If you asked her, Brenda would tell you that she thinks a tour of military service" (or actually any service such as the Peace Corp, Teach for America or church organized mission service) "would prove beneficial for a lot of young persons between the ages of eighteen and twenty-one who want to work but find it hard to get a job. She points out that in a way the military is a restricted community. 'But with that comes a sense of stability, and with this stability a chance to make a sound decision as to what you want to do in life, be it as military or civilian,'" Brenda shared in an interview with SSgt. Daniel L. Smith in his article in *Military Honors* titled, "Brenda Newberry: Competition Serves to Help Us Grow and Develop."

If you aren't in over your head, how do you know how tall you are?
– T.S. Eliot

Towards the end of our final year in Spain, I was transferred to the supply training unit and began to assist with managing technical training and testing. During this time, I created and posted a daily training tip for base supply airmen to assist them with understanding, learning, and incorporating into their work the required processes, regulations, and rules. Each day, I posted a different tip or advice to improve training knowledge. The result was an increase in the numbers that passed the technical exam, thereby increasing eligibility for promotions.

In the Air Force, promotions were not easy. It was not just grade and time in service, but there was also a subjective component determined by the superiors as well as the "need" component which represented the overall Air Force determination of the number of personnel required each year in each skill, specialty, and grade. However, passing and maintaining technical expertise was critical. It was the measurable improvements to the technical competency of base supply personnel that garnered the recognition of my superior. Upon reflection, my superior also recognized other attributes or there is no way I could have won the top Air Force honor for enlisted personnel.

Making the improvements in the squadron testing performance, teamed with exemplary past performance while assigned to the receiving department running a Univac-1050 remote system and keypunch machine, successfully going to the university, consistently making the Dean's list, and community involvement with the dance "troupe," led to me being nominated and selected as Unit, Squadron, Division, Base, and ultimately United States Air Forces in Europe (USAFE) Airman of the year.

The Outstanding Airman of the Year is a military award of the United States Air Force recognizing twelve outstanding enlisted service members who demonstrate superior leadership, job performance, community involvement, and personal achievement. The Outstanding Airman of the

Year is the highest personal ribbon award of the United States Air Force for enlisted personnel. It was with the major command, United States Air Forces in Europe, that I was recognized with the honor.

Brenda and Maurice Outstanding Airmen of the Year Award
Ceremony 1978

One had to successfully pass reviews and interviews with a selection board at each level (Unit, Squadron, Division, and Major Command) in order to advance to the next. This included the Chief Master Sergeant of the Air Force, a general officer, and selected Major command chiefs form the selection board for the top award. The Air Force Chief of Staff reviews the selections before they are confirmed.

From a field of 570,000 candidates that year, I was selected as one of the twelve Outstanding Airmen of the year 1978, representing the Major Command United States Air Forces in Europe.

It was quite an honor and I received much press as well as an all-expense paid trip to Ramstein Air Base in Germany, which included a tour of East and West Berlin, for the European recognition. This was followed by a trip to Washington, D.C. from Scott Air Force Base in Belleville, Illinois, where we were assigned after Spain. Maurice, as my spouse, was able to accompany me to Washington, D.C., where we met the other twelve honorees as well as many Air Force and Department of Defense dignitaries such as the Secretary of the Air Force, John Stetson, and Secretary of Defense, Harold Brown. It was a new situation in those days when the spouse was the husband, but Maurice handled it gracefully and with strong support. I often tell people that Maurice was and always has been secure in his masculinity.

After being in Spain for three and a half years, we requested to be assigned to California, Georgia, Florida or some other warm place. Instead, we were assigned to Scott Air Force Base in Belleville, Illinois. Neither of us wanted to be in Illinois, but it was closer to our parents and closer to our "home of record" for the Air Force.

I remember getting out of the car that very warm late June day and commenting to Maurice, "Wow! This must be how hades feels." It was stifling humidity without any breeze, which I later realized was the norm for summers in that part of the country. It was strange getting back to the U.S. because we had not returned at all during those years in Spain. We were well received on base because news had spread of my having been awarded the honor of being one of the twelve Outstanding Airmen for the year 1978. Their local newspaper did a spread on Maurice and me, citing that we were a couple whose teamwork was instrumental.

The Newberrys say it is important that they both be accepted, writes Metro-East Journal reporter Jean Ann Bailey (September 14, 1978). "They accepted us as a team, they should be able to keep us as a team," Brenda said. Maurice said they have remained together during their enlistment because of a joint spouse assignment program, although it looked at one time as if they might be separated.

Neither is there any professional jealousy between her and her husband. "Sure we're competitive," says Maurice, "but our competition serves to help us grow and develop." He added, "As Black persons, we have sometimes found that it is not always enough to do just your job, so Brenda and I have always strived to be better than average."

At home the teamwork continues. As Brenda puts it, "We talk a lot. Communication with each other is essential. Since we both put in nine hours on the job, we tend to share things when we get home. If one cooks, the other washes dishes."

"And if one is tired, the other does both," adds Maurice.

Looking back at the achievements and hearing the strong determination in their voices, you get the feeling that the Newberrys truly do have a bright future ahead of them. No matter the challenge, they are confident of overcoming it—together.

Entering a Whole New Phase

We had also successfully applied for Officer Training and were looking forward to attending Officer's Training School (OTS), but that was not God's will. I discovered that I was with child, which thrilled my grandmother who accused us of being selfish when we chose not to conceive even after six years of marriage. The policy at that time was that I would have to re-apply to OTS so rather than being separated, we elected to go forward with our honorable discharge as per our enlistment rather than remaining in the Air Force. At that time, there was not a pregnancy uniform, so the transition to become more "female friendly" had not yet occurred.

Our first child was born at the base hospital in March and we were due for discharge in June. Actually, while not the original plan, it was perfect. We had sixty days of vacation saved, so I did not have to return to work on base after giving birth. Our active duty ended in June, but Maurice had found employment with McDonnell Douglas by May.

Civilian life was quite different. Our living costs were much higher. There was no commissary or base store. I remember our first grocery bill being more than double! With a new baby, life was definitely more difficult. Diapers were not cheap!

Because our apartment was small and the owner did not want children, we had to move. Since the work was in St. Louis, we prepared for that move. We would call several apartment complexes that allowed children before driving over to St. Louis to ensure they had availability. Though they said they had three or more apartments available, when we arrived, one look at us and suddenly they had no apartments available. Interesting treatment for 1979.

We also noticed that several retail and grocery store clerks would not place our change in our hands. (Those were the days when people would still carry and pay with cash.) It was surprising and amazing to us! After being in Spain so long and dealing with diverse ethnic groups in the Air Force, being in St. Louis was like going back to the mindset of the fifties or earlier with respect to various aspects of race relations.

As I look at the rage, demonstrations, and riots reported in the media about a St. Louis suburb, Ferguson, and later Berkley in August through December 2014, I strongly believe that it was not just the distorted reporting of police and the killing of young Black men, but about the deeper rampant, institutionalized, and unrealized racism by the white majority. Racism was so obviously prevalent in the region to anyone that had lived in other cities or countries.

In reflecting on my own experiences in that region, it is very probable that the demonstrators were expressing years of mistreatment, poor schools, few to no jobs, exclusion from higher level positions in spite of qualifications, being treated without respect, targeted, redlined, and just plain made to feel as if there was no hope because of the extreme poverty in their neighborhoods. Granted, conversely, Blacks must learn to respect authority, maintain family structures, stay in school and actually learn, attend college, technical school, and/or obtain skills following high school graduation, commit no crimes, resist drug and alcohol abuse, maintain a "moral compass," and seek to become contributing members of society. In spite of what we experienced in the St. Louis region, we had hope because of the foundation of family, education, travel, strong faith in God, discipline achieved through service, and solid employable skills.

Armed with undergrad and graduate degrees, we proceeded to make the St. Louis region home. Finally, we found a townhouse west of St. Louis in the city of Ellisville. I stayed home with our daughter, but after six months Maurice knew something was wrong. I acted strangely and uncharacteristically dependent. When I called Maurice at work to ask him if I could buy shampoo, he realized something was definitely wrong. We realized I had a calling to go back to work outside of the home. We came into agreement that it was good for me and our family, so I applied at McDonnell Douglas, was given an offer of employment, found a terrific babysitter, and started work within two weeks.

Less than one week later, we were informed that the townhouses we were living in were being converted to condos, and we would have to either purchase it or move before it was time to renew the lease. We chose to buy a home. Thankfully, I had already begun working outside the home, so we were poised to save in preparation for the home purchase.

We worked with a recommended realtor for several weeks, but noticed a pattern in that she only took us to Black neighborhoods. Not accepting that housing limitation after so many years of being treated as simply "human" while in the Air Force, we ventured out on our own and ended up building a new home in St. Peters, Missouri, which was even further west than Ellisville, but only about twelve miles from work. Unfortunately, we did not recognize how truly segregated the region was and found manure thrown on the garage door soon after we moved in.

When we would ride bikes with our daughter on the back of mine, we sometimes would get fast food drink cups thrown at us. The person would holler that "N" word at us while they rapidly drive off. As late as the 1990s, our mailbox would often get targeted and hit. We finally put up a brick encased mailbox so at least they would damage their car as well if they chose to continue this destructive activity.

When our daughter started preschool she came home and asked if she was bad. When we inquired, she indicated that the kids teased her saying she, "was black and black kids are bad."

Later that summer, I visited a neighborhood pool with her and when we got in the water, everyone else exited. No, it was not a pool break time. They just got out. When we left the water, they re-entered the pool. This was in 1981! Fortunately, our daughter was too young to be aware of such treatment.

It was then we realized that we had to be selective in her education, so we proceeded to investigate alternatives to the ignorance and prejudice that we believed would be expressed and experienced in the local public schools. I also shared with Maurice a dream that became a goal to purchase our own pool so our daughter would never experience that type of humiliation at a time in which she was aware of that kind of racial treatment. Thanks to the Lord, our hard work paid off and we did get an in-ground pool installed in our backyard by 1988.

Daughters Enjoying Pool Time

We also put our daughter on the list for the local private Catholic elementary school because we believed that, while there would be some degree of prejudice, it would be less acceptable in that environment. She was accepted as was our youngest daughter. We were correct about the acceptability of prejudice attitudes, at least until high school. In her freshman year of high school, our oldest daughter overheard hall conversation commenting that they could not believe the school "let in" another Black. This was in 1993!

We stayed the course because running away for us was and had never been an option. It was extremely important that we raise our daughters with a strong sense of self-worth, no bitterness when confronted with racism, and the strength to take responsibility for life outcomes. Like our parents, we did not accept a victim mentality. Blaming others was not an answer that was acceptable for our family. Searching for ways to work around situations and tactfully dealing with them was the process we chose for our lives.

If our girls complained about a grade received, we counseled them to respectfully inquire of the teacher exactly what they had not done correctly so they would understand how to do better on the next paper or exam. Usually, the disparity only occurred for the subjective portions of the paper or exam. My experience led me to believe that teachers were less able to exercise subconscious or conscious prejudice or preconceptions regarding the lack of intelligence Blacks possessed on multiple choice and true or false questions. So, directly talking with the teacher to understand their subjective expectations was important and often made the difference between an "A" grade and "B" grade. As a result, both girls were great students and received scholarships to college.

I found that the same approach is important as one deals with the business or corporate "world" as well. Following processes, policies, and rules is important, but understanding the subjective expectations by talking to the boss periodically about your career and going "above and beyond" is critical for success. That is a critical and key element that many people miss. It is important to follow the processes, policies, and rules rather than trying to find ways around them. Secondly, it is equally important to talk with your boss and managers to determine what is viewed as important for success and then follow up often to ensure you are on track.

Lessons at Work

At McDonnell Douglas, I worked as a logistics engineer where we planned the movement and inventory of aircraft equipment from first delivery through obsolescence. I was the only female in the group and also the youngest. An older gentleman, became a mentor and also taught me some lessons about operating in a political business environment which was quite unlike the military.

I remember him noting at one point that both he and his parents were college graduates. He then noted that I was a first generation college graduate and the granddaughter of a sharecropper.

"Wow!" he said, "And you are sitting here working right next to me. I don't know if that makes me less or you more."

Quite an interesting perspective that I thought about often as I learned the ins and outs of working in civilian life. In fact, that may be the reason for such racial tension centuries after slavery and decades after the civil rights era. When some Whites see Blacks doing well or even better educationally and economically, they may have the same thoughts that he expressed. Given the difficulties and disadvantages Blacks had and still experience in America, Whites may wonder are they less for not having achieved more because they do not and did not have to deal with negativity, prejudice, and adversity or should they be glad to see the progress of the nation with a growing number of Blacks doing well?

It is a conflicting situation that may lead to resentment or guilt. Are they somehow less because someone Black is doing equally well or does it mean that someone Black must have excelled given the adversities they had to overcome to be "in the same place." After all, intellect tells us that the more educated, employed, and contributing adults there are, the better for the entire country.

In the beginning, he was always available to offer us advice. When we were looking for our home, he advised us to purchase the most and best home we could afford.

"Find one you could live in for thirty years or more if necessary," he advised.

Like us, he believed that it was freeing not to have a mortgage, so rather than moving "up" every five years as many people did at that time, he was in a home that met his needs, was fully paid off, and beautiful. We listened to that advice and not only stayed in the home we built for over thirty years, we also successfully paid it off in sixteen years. It was excellent advice which ultimately gave us tremendous peace and flexibility when we first started our own business and beyond.

After we took his advice and bought the most and best home we could afford, he drove by and later expressed how my home was bigger and better than his. He also compared salaries and then became envious when early on I was selected to travel to Washington, D.C. NAVAIR headquarters to meet with our Navy counterparts. He allowed his jealousy to interfere with what had

I learned that many people constantly compare themselves with others which can lead to a negative instead of a positive relationship.

started out as a productive work relationship. He sometimes would purposely give me incorrect information so he could point out what I did wrong. He became less friendly and definitely moved to a position of competitiveness. I did not feel competitive to him or even others, only myself. My goal was not to beat him or anyone else, only to do my best so I would not get fired. After all, we had family goals to achieve.

I tend to observe and admire others with an interest to determine how to achieve what they have achieved, but not from a vantage point of envy. I met and knew many "successful" people who were materially wealthy, extremely kind, faithful, and good. I viewed them with admiration, not jealousy or anger. My goal has always been to grow and become better at whatever I put my mind to do in life. Learning from others was an important part of that goal.

I also learned that as an African American female, it was best not to share too much because those that compare and are envious can and sometimes will make things difficult for you at work so that you are not able to progress. Such was the politics of human behavior in the competitive corporate environment—unfortunate but true. Later, I would enter business entrepreneurship, thankful for the lessons I learned.

Nuggets for Living Fully and Successfully

Maurice and I learned the value of working together as a team and meeting life's challenges head on. Check off the ones you are already successfully doing and circle those you may need to work on.

- No professional jealousy should exist between husband and wife.
- Let your competition serve to help you grow and develop.
- Comparing yourself to the performance of others at work probably will not push you to excellence. Developing a mindset to be excellent, go beyond your best, and exceed expectations will serve you much better than comparing yourself to others.
- Always strive to be better than average.
- Talk a lot to your spouse. Communication with each other is essential.

- No matter the challenge, remain confident of overcoming it—together.
- Stay the course. Running away is usually not a good option.
- Persevering with a positive attitude through problems and prejudice will ultimately develop a character shaped by courage, graciousness, and forgiveness.
- Do not accept a victim mentality. Blaming others is not an answer.
- Searching for ways to work around situations and tactfully deal with them is the process to follow.
- Observe and admire others with an interest to determine how to achieve what they have achieved. Not from a vantage point of envy, but from a vantage point of life lessons.
- Make it your goal to grow and become better at whatever you are doing.

If you start to think the problem is out there stop yourself. That thought is the problem.   – Steven Covey

The Real Payoff (St. Louis Commerce Magazine, July 2004 by Glen Sparks)

"I teasingly call it a midlife crisis," says Newberry, 52. "Sometimes you just reach a crossroads. I had been [at MasterCard] for twelve years and I wanted to do something different. Really, the higher you go up in a company, the fewer openings there are."

Chapter 5

ACCIDENTAL ENTREPRENEUR-THE START

Don't waste time learning the "tricks of the trade." Instead, learn the trade. – H. Jackson Brown, Jr. "Life's Little Instruction Book"

People often ask why I started the business. They ask if it was a childhood or adult dream. Honestly, it was never a thought and I truly believe it was a path directed by God. The reason is multifold. I could not have preplanned many of the elements that were important for positioning me or the business for relevance in the year it began and beyond. The only planning was the understanding of the importance of hard work, integrity, and character.

In 1987, while at MasterCard, I received the opportunity to teach undergraduate and graduate courses in operating systems and network management at Washington University in St. Louis. I ended up doing this for over twenty years. Working with computers in the Air Force, at McDonnell Douglas, and MasterCard positioned me to accept this challenge. Little did I know it would later add to my credibility as an entrepreneur.

Who could have known being a veteran and working for McDonnell Douglas, a major defense contractor, would later be important for understanding how a business should interface with government agencies or that being veteran-owned was a business benefit? Who would have known that being stationed in Spain would position one for later interfacing globally for business when later working for MasterCard International and traveling to Europe and South America? Who could have known that being assigned to base supply running remote systems or keypunch machines would become a future job, career, and business in information technology? Computers were not mainstream in the mid-seventies.

Who could have known that entertaining myself by learning the keyboard as a twelve year old would make me extremely effective later in using the computer keyboard in almost everything we do when there were not even computers anywhere around at the time, at least not in my world? Working, learning, and developing all of these life skills, building character through challenges, and day-to-day work throughout the years were not necessarily "fun," special or important, but later they all became part of the important whole for a "successful" career, business, and life. Just functioning very well with life in 2015 requires a certain degree of computer and cyber security competency. From Cable TV to smart devices to washing machines and dryers, they all have some form of computer technology.

In the Air Force I had the reinforcement of all the family and Christian values and obtained skills as well. In the '70s, it was not politically incorrect for the Air Force or other public entities to support Christian values, so even that experience supported the values derived from family and church. What added to the early values I was taught was that mission "trumps" the individual, and teamwork does not require 100 percent melding of personalities. Also, a determination to work together to accomplish the mission, and all commitments must be honored no matter how difficult.

When I was promoted to be a vice president of a profit and loss business unit at MasterCard International, after the right amount of congratulations, Maurice asked me, "How many vice presidents have been at MasterCard longer than five years?"

After thinking about it, I had to truthfully say, "There was only one." It seemed to be that corporate politics either encouraged them to take job opportunities elsewhere, be assigned to "special projects" which was then the code word for not of use anymore, or their division was reorganized leaving them no position and no choice but to leave. Either way, that level did not have long lasting staying power at the time.

> In hindsight, the values from God, family, and military were great foundations. When teamed with the path followed, it is obvious that it was not planned by a human.

He then said that we need to tighten up and get our financial house in order so there would be options should we need them in the future. Now we were always frugal buying things on sale, cooking meals at home, and making lunches for the kids and for ourselves to take to work. We also did not take extravagant vacations. This was because most of our funds were used for the basics, working towards paying off the mortgage, and the extremely important education of our children.

Steven Covey, in his writing, comments that we need to "begin with the end in mind." So in all aspects of life, it is important to think through and determine possible or future next steps. For example, even though we have in our society the term "permanent job," nothing is permanent. Prepare for your next position or job by learning, contributing, and involvement in as many areas as you are able to absorb. By constantly growing, you will be prepared when that day of change comes and you have to move on.

It is impossible to think of every possible scenario, but it is important not to just meander through life or the deviations and changes that challenge you or you will be devastated rather than exhilarated.

Four years after the promotion, the time of decision arrived just as Maurice had predicted. My boss was a very kind and fair, yet he was also a very tough man. He was the person that selected me to transfer from the technical side to director of a business unit and subsequently promoted me to vice president. However, he lived and worked in the New York offices and was a bit of what many would describe as a stereotypical New Yorker—a bit brash and impatient. That did not bother me, but many of my peers and his peers did not care for him. Often in meetings they would talk negatively about him.

When I started out with MasterCard, there were less than 180 people in the entire company. Promotions and opportunity were based on performance. There was little time for politics. By the time I was promoted to vice president, there were over 1200 people. A new group of people were hired into key high level positions from a major Kansas City telecommunications firm with a substantial difference in corporate culture. Some of them at higher levels seemed to be of the mindset that getting ahead was about highlighting or making others look bad rather than by improving their own performance.

Respecting my boss, I would listen but not get involved in the negative comments because my basic nature was not to "trash" my boss. I felt and practiced the belief that the way to get rid of a bad boss was to make the boss look as good as possible. Do their work for them and let them sign and take credit for the work you did for them. This, of course, is in addition to your own work. These actions should position the boss for promotion or cause the boss to seek other employment worthy of their talents. The boss will remember who "took care of them" and will probably recommend you to take their place or recommend you for a promotion elsewhere.

If that fails, the foundation and lessons that you learned will have positioned you to seek other opportunities yourself. Either way, eventually you will get a new boss without compromising personal character and work ethics. It may take time, but patience is often a necessary element in preparation to accomplish future goals. However, if the environment becomes too toxic, unethical, unlawful or immoral it is important to exercise your judgement and seek other opportunities at the earliest appropriate time for you.

One day while peers were "trashing" my boss at a meeting I joined in! I was immediately convicted and felt the environment of the negative oriented culture was "rubbing off" on me. It was not a place I wanted to be and felt it was not reflective of my belief and integrity. I was not afraid or concerned about being fired or the like because I was an excellent worker and the company needed to have diversity at my level—I was it at the time. However, my integrity was of great importance to me. I knew I had only joined in for acceptance.

I had often thought it was important to reflect on how the negative and positive behavior of yourself or others will naturally spiral attitudes and treatment of others upward or downward. For example, if you knowingly let a child steal a piece of candy, next time it might be a bag of chips or a soft drink, and later in life their stealing could get to the point they are committing grand larceny. Opening the door to what is negative even a crack can gradually desensitize us to fit into the forming negative culture. I did not want to become a part of what I saw as a new culture.

As a result, I went home that evening and told Maurice that I thought it was time for me to resign. It was the final straw to what had been building up to this moment. The other critical thing that also contributed to this decision was the way in which I worked.

Because I always endeavored to give my all as if for God, I would often go into the office at 7:30 a.m. in the morning and work until 1:00 a.m. the next morning. Only recently I learned that the long and late hours impacted our younger daughter when she shared with me that she would stay awake at night worried about me getting home safely. I would always go into our daughters' rooms to check on them and kiss them once I got home no matter what time it was. When I arrived home and would come into her room to check on her, she would pretend to be asleep. So my long hours did take a toll on my family more than I realized at the time.

There was also much travel involved. Maurice was quite supportive even to the point of learning to braid our daughter's hair. We always ensured one or both of us were with the kids, but my promotion to vice president was quite a bit more demanding.

We had customer banks worldwide which meant that not only were the hours long, there was substantial travel required as well. I was so available that we had a couple of customers in Asia contact my boss upset because I did not answer a call at 2:00 a.m. central time which would have been 5:00 p.m. there. He kindly reminded them of the time zone and counseled me that I had set an unrealistic expectation of availability, one that he had not required but that I had created due to my desire to be exceptional. Those lessons from parents of having to work harder and be better just to be equal continued to be part of my psyche.

My business travel was exciting as I flew first or business class to destinations such as Puerto Rico, Santiago, Chile, Bogota, Columbia, Caracas, Venezuela, Brussels, Belgium, and many places in the US such as San Francisco, San Diego, New York, Boston, Miami, etc. I was functional in Spanish due to our Air Force years in Spain, so I enjoyed the varied cultural experiences immensely. It was interesting and I met many interesting people. Seldom, if ever, were there other women and certainly no African Americans, so I felt that I had to do above and beyond what was expected. It was not about me, but the possible positive impact I could have on others when I performed well. My performance could be the reason they gave other women or minorities an opportunity or the reason they would not. We both felt the sacrifice was worth it until I began to really miss out on important family events.

Maurice had become a coach for the girls' track team at our daughter's high school in order to monitor how they were treated and to support their involvement. There was a track banquet to be held at our home. I was to fly back home from San Francisco that Friday afternoon so that I could be there. Well, a client in San Diego had some problems and I needed to travel there to assist in the relationship. Needless to say, I did not make the original flight and the flight out of San Diego was late delaying my arrival home to 10:30 p.m. I was tired, frustrated, and devastated to have missed the track event. Though my family was calm and everyone was peaceful and not angry, I was sorely disappointed I had missed everything.

Then when I learned all they had gone through to successfully pull off the event without me, I was even more upset. When picking up the food Maurice locked his keys in the car, had to call our daughter to stop by home, pick up the extra set of keys, and get them to him. They barely made it back home in time, set everything up, and it all went well. In spite of their challenges, no one was angry with me. In fact, they all acted as if I was not even missed, but I knew I had missed an important event in my daughter's life!

So the hours I had to put in to properly serve the worldwide clients (who had become accustomed to getting in touch with me day or night), teamed with the travel, missing important family events, and the risk to my own character and integrity, resulted in the decision to resign. The trashing of the boss was the final straw for which I could no longer justify any of my other sacrifices.

Four years before, in preparation for this day, we had worked together to become more financially sound, so Maurice's response was a simple, "Okay, if you are sure." The next morning I turned in my resignation. That early financial and professional preparation created the foundation that resulted in an easy decision.

Though we were prepared for this change, when I resigned I did not have a plan for the work I would do next. Starting a business was not a goal. There were no close entrepreneurial role models in my life at the time. In fact, I had been taught to get an education, get a good professional position, and work all my life preferably for a prestigious organization or company.

Tom, a wonderful friend who had worked in Human Resources at MasterCard and now had his own consulting firm, called and wanted to work with me to find another position when he heard I had resigned. He had me interview for a couple of high level positions, but I was concerned about the various environments and people working in positions under those levels thinking they should have the job. I did not want to be part of a new organization's corporate politics and negativity that would resemble what I had begun to experience at MasterCard.

Knowing that MasterCard was not unique in corporate politics, and doing research on the various corporations I was interviewing for, I learned they too were void of black male or female high level executives and board of directors. It was obvious I would be experiencing similar or worse politics and negativity. Some of those having to report to me would be either consciously or unconsciously resentful of having to report to a minority female. It was different at MasterCard where the resentment did not appear until much later. This is probably because when I started working there, the total number of employees was less than 180. That meant many of us had "grown" together professionally and gained trust and respect for each other. As newer people were hired, many came from dysfunctional organizations and they created or preferred dysfunction, negativity, and backstabbing.

While moving up the corporate ladder, I had situations in which it appeared as if I was invisible, such as watching others less qualified and with less education obtain promotions over me. Situations such as being in meetings and having no one comment after something I suggested as if I had not talked at all or making a comment that was ignored only to have someone else, usually a white male, make the exact same or slightly reworded comment moments later and see everyone embrace it. As I grew more confident and more disturbed by these events, I began to let those in the meeting know that I had made the very same comment earlier. There were also times when those that reported to me would talk to me about others just to see what I would say so they could go back and report or gossip.

I had to constantly ask and note what was required in order to be promoted or positioned for the next level. Once I received the information from my boss, it was important that I achieve the skill, obtain the certification or acquire the knowledge necessary for consideration for the promotion or next level. Once achieved, it was important to then touch base with the boss again to ensure they were aware of it. When the boss was too busy to complete my performance appraisal, I found it useful to complete my own appraisal and give it to the boss so they only had to edit and add their own facts. What better way to ensure your achievements were noted?

I also discovered that often there was a "meeting before the meeting" in which the person with the key agenda contacted some of the attendees to explain the situation, answer questions, and obtain their agreement before the meeting. Often I would naively be sitting in the meeting and observe that everyone was in agreement without much discussion and wonder what I had missed. Later I found out I was not privy and had not been included in the "meeting before the meeting" so I missed the key elements of background information, a situation often specifically experienced by minorities and females. Learning how to be included in these pre-meetings was important so I would not make the business political mistake of seeming uninformed or ignorant by seeking more information and discussion during the actual meeting.

When mentoring those new to business, I often share this concept with them because it is very important for career development. Conversely, if you are the one with the key agenda, it is important to have pre-meetings to ensure most are in agreement rather than waiting for the actual meeting. It saves time, prevents the embarrassment that might occur if you were not prepared for some of the questions during the meeting, and provides for smooth execution of the meeting agenda. It was a concept never shared with me, one I learned the hard way through experience.

It was a tough journey. The long hours and performance were based on my parents' constant refrain that I had to be better and work harder. They taught me not to complain, but just concentrate on doing my best. They let me know that I could not do what "white people" did if I wanted to be successful. I had to follow the rules and excel just to be even.

Based on my experiences and beliefs, I decided not to pursue other corporate executive positions and had no interest in taking positions at lower levels. After all, I had worked hard to achieve the level acquired and did not want to go backwards.

It was interesting and sounded like a challenge which I always enjoyed. It also presented an option without the drama of working for someone else. Knowing I needed input from my husband before making a decision of that magnitude, I went home and discussed it with Maurice.

His response was, "Well, you aren't doing anything now. Might as well give it a try."

So, that is what I did. Doing the research to determine the method, I realized Tom was right! I had basically run a standalone profit and loss business unit at MasterCard which is

Finally Tom said, "You have the background, education, ability and intellect, why don't you just start your own IT consulting firm?"

very much like a small business, but with established clients and an established reputation. I understood marketing, customer service, branding, technology, and was definitely not afraid of hard work.

So the journey into the world of small business began. All the hard work, positions, opportunities, and travel from the past were great foundations for owning and running a small business. They all intersected for such a time as this making me realize it was all part of God's divine plan for my life. I have discovered that when life suddenly hits me with the "unexpected," I need to step back and review all that has led up to that moment. Why? Because God may well have used where I have been to prepare me for just that moment and given me both the experience and wisdom to know what to do next.

Thomas Jefferson said, "I am a great believer in luck and I find the harder I work the more luck I have."

Accidental Strength

As I looked back at this divine plan, I realized there were many events that led me to this moment in time. Sometimes events with challenges prepare us for greater strength in the future. Two such events were the births of our two daughters.

Our first child was born a mere three months prior to the end of our enlistment. That meant I did not have to return to work following her birth. I was on maternity leave and then vacation following our honorable discharge. While we definitely were aware that we wanted to be parents, the impact of not being able to attend Officer's Training School changed our career and family plans immensely. God threw us into a different path altogether. He used the birth of our first child to not only change our life path, but also to strengthen and prepare me for the journey ahead.

Our first daughter was born at the Air Force Base hospital and it was a natural childbirth using the Lamaze method with no drugs. Perhaps Lamaze or natural childbirth was encouraged for parent and newborn health or perhaps to simply save money, but either way I was convinced. We had taken Lamaze classes so that natural childbirth was an option. When I went into labor in the afternoon, we headed to the hospital. I was admitted and labor continued, but slowed down a bit. It was very cold in the hospital and I was not comfortable. Since my labor had slowed down, they sent us home that evening.

In the Air Force back in those days, we had to work until delivery. Therefore, I was determined not to go back to the cold uncomfortable hospital and lose sleep if there was a chance I would be going to work the next day! So, I continued Lamaze breathing through the night and stayed nice and warm at home while lightly sleeping until I felt the urge to push. From those Lamaze classes, I knew the various key "indicators" and the urge to push was a key indicator.

We rushed to the hospital around 2:20 a.m. Immediately after entering the hospital, my water broke and Maurice was told to hurry and park the car because the baby was not waiting. He barely made it into the delivery room. She was born at 2:44 a.m. There was no time to request any form of pain medication. So having natural childbirth was a result of my decision to stay comfortable during early labor rather than some unique strength or determination to have a baby naturally.

Interestingly, it was a bit different with our second and final child, also a girl. I had prepared by reading refreshers on Lamaze, but the book that really made a difference was "The Immaculate Deception." This book highlighted the natural process of childbirth within the farm animal "community." The author noted that the animals seemed to go into a deep form of relaxation, sort of a light sleep so the body could relax all muscles except those at work for childbirth. The concepts very closely resembled the Lamaze teachings with an added twist.

The author also warned about allowing Pitocin during labor which is often introduced for the convenience of the attendant shifts to increase contractions and speed up delivery, but at the same time it makes the pain much greater. The author highlighted stories of hospital staff using Pitocin to ensure the birth before the end of their shift or to ensure it was time to deliver by the time the doctor arrived so the doctor would not have to wait and could get on with his or her day. The use of Pitocin often then led to the need to get an epidural to ease the painful contractions the Pitocin had caused.

As a result, at night I would practice deep relaxation including full relaxing of all muscles. I certainly did not want an epidural or Pitocin since I made it through the first childbirth without it. Also, after reading the book and reviewing the Lamaze techniques, I wanted to fully experience the birth. We had just returned from our oldest daughter's gymnastic classes when labor started. When labor began, I began Lamaze breathing and relaxing. Our four and half-year-old daughter stood beside me coaching me and assisting me in breathing.

In civilian life, child delivery was quite different. They encouraged epidurals and other "drugs." I was not allowed to work until my due date or beyond for insurance and safety reasons and had to stop working two weeks before the due date. This impacted our financial planning, but was beyond our control. Given the situation, the baby had to be born on the due date or we would be financially impacted. I also noted that the hospital was quite different. I had a private room! Yippee!

After admission, contractions continued and became stronger. I was able to fall into deep relaxation because of the months of practice and preparation. Maurice watched TV peacefully, but was on guard because we had instructed the hospital staff that no Pitocin was to be introduced without our permission. When the doctor came in, he was surprised that I was so calm while in the final stages of labor. He asked the nurses what was going on because he could not believe it was so calm in the room. Maurice had plenty of time to put on the scrubs to participate with the birth in the delivery room. Bottom line, in a couple of hours the baby was born right on my mother's birthday. She was immediately placed on my chest where she began nursing. It was a very peaceful birth experience.

This time I was prepared and purposely chose to deliver naturally. The peace I experienced through these strength building events was something I would remember all through my life's journey, not only in the business world, but during future physical challenges as well. I would need peace and strength for surviving the challenges that would soon present themselves.

Nuggets for Living Fully and Successfully

In my St. Charles Community College Commencement Speech, May 15, 2010, I challenged the graduates then and offer the same challenge to you today:

In many graduation speeches, the speaker encourages the graduates to be of service. Please note, that I ask that you be of excellence wherever you are because that is the greatest service you can give. Each person is provided gifts and must use them with excellence. Not everyone is meant to serve as a missionary, in public service, in third world countries, in the Peace Corp or other very sacrificing services. But service is using your gifts at your appointed place in time, all of the time, and to the best of your ability. You can bring value and help to others right in your circle of influence wherever that may be. As you move forward on your path using your gifts, please don't disrespect or be against others that you may perceive as doing better or worse. You see, they have different gifts and paths....

There are several key principles I would like you to take away from this chapter that will help you with the challenges you will face in the journey of your life:

➢ "Don't waste time learning the 'tricks of the trade.' Instead, learn the trade." List skills that you have learned or enhanced over the past year or two. List new skills you need to learn or enhance in the next year to prepare for your future.

➢ Core planning involves understanding the importance of hard work, integrity, and character. Are you including these elements in your planning?

➢ Hard work, positions, opportunities, and travel from the past were great foundations that can all intersect demonstrating that they are part of God's divine plan. List some areas of your life that you realize have set the foundation for your paths.

➤ Mission "trumps" the individual, teamwork does not require 100 percent melding of personalities just a determination to work together to accomplish the mission, and all commitments must be honored no matter how difficult. Ensure that you live up to and honor your commitments.

➤ Thomas Jefferson said: "I am a great believer in luck and I find the harder I work the more luck I have." Think of areas in your life in which focused hard work has led to luck. What are areas in which you need more focused attention and work?

➤ Events with challenges often prepare us for greater strength in the future. View your challenges as opportunities. What opportunities are you now prepared and ready to go after?

Review past challenges and trials when facing new ones. You can learn from them about how life and God has prepared you for your next step.

What It Takes – *St. Louis Remains a Hostile Environment for Small, Minority-Owned Firms. Here's How to Succeed Anyway* (St. Louis Small Business Monthly/August 2011 by Jeremy Nulik)

**"They told me, 'You're going to try to start up as a woman and a minority firm specializing in IT? It will never be successful. Too much competition.'
They doubted I would make it," says Newberry.**

Chapter 6

SURVIVING THE CHALLENGES

"**A** smart **man learns** from **his mistakes**, but a brilliant **man** watches others and **learns** from their **mistakes**." (Russian proverb)

I have noticed the tendency of our youth in the United States and perhaps other developed countries, to put more stock in what their peers say rather than listening to the advice and wisdom of elders. The technology seems to drive this because many elders are at a loss with regard to technology. Therefore, the youth share information and advice with peers using the technology and social media. The problem is that often their peers are in the same or worse situation and have no "real" life experience with the long-term results and consequences of decisions and actions. I strongly believe that in spite of a lack of technical savvy, elders have survived the challenges and their advice definitely has credence.

For instance, sixty-year-old smokers who are being treated for lung cancer should be a testament to not smoking. One who drank alcohol excessively and is now being treated for colon or other related cancers and suffered social, family, and emotional problems is a testament to the dangers of excessive alcohol. As a newlywed, I would much rather take marriage advice from a couple that has actually been married fifty years than friends or peers married only five years.

When it came to starting my own business, I talked to people that had achieved my desired vision and asked them questions to understand how they had achieved success rather than asking my peers who were in the same place in life. Want to retire at fifty-five? Read about it and ask as many people as possible how they did it. You will find many underlying themes of universal wisdom. While you may not be able to "copy" what they did, you may be able to derive similar character traits and values to move you along that path. Want to raise "successful" independent children? Talk to and read about those that have. Why go to child psychologists that have studied but never raised any children?

Dot the "i's" and Cross the "t's"

It seems that nothing was ever enough. No matter what I had or accomplished somehow it was not sufficient. Potential clients always wanted more qualifications before they would hire my firm. Starting a business is tough for anyone, but like most people, I believed it was tougher for me. Statistics say 80 percent of small businesses do not get past two years and 80 percent of those do not reach year five. So just surviving is a challenge. Thriving it seems takes an act of Divine guidance and intervention.

I started the business with nothing except a solid education, graduate degree in business, a background as an Air Force Veteran, and over thirty-five years of direct information technology experience. Additionally, it was the mid '90s and technology was "hot," the economy was growing very well, and business startups were getting lots of traction with the ever growing internet landscape. We personally had an excellent credit rating, no mortgage, and solid savings. Rather than coming on board right away,

Maurice continued to work so we had sufficient income to support our family needs during our business startup phase.

Like anyone starting a business should do, I sought resources that could help me learn more. The SBA was exceptional and the staff was extremely helpful especially once they realized my determination. After attending several seminars with the Small Business Administration (SBA) and SCORE (Service Corp of Retired Executives), I completed a business plan and went to the bank to obtain a small loan. To demonstrate how small the loan we were applying for really was, the amount requested was only a portion of what we had in our savings account. Well, I was disappointed because the bank turned me down, but agreed to take the entire loan amount requested from our savings and place it into a five year CD as collateral.

I was also disappointed because I had heard of others getting loans of much greater amounts than we requested with a much shallower background and massive other debt. Why the bank we had done business with for over twenty years would not give us the small loan requested was beyond me. Why they could not see the great potential based on the many years of demonstrated character, integrity, and professionalism was a major disappointment.

Since we majored in business, had thirty-five years of experience, maintained a household with excellent credit ratings and solid financials for over twenty-four years, it was not rocket science for us to realize we could simply loan ourselves the funds from our own savings to begin our business instead of borrowing from the bank. Of course, we had to follow all the rules of keeping business and personal accounting separate, and ensuring the loan terms were legal and correct within all required government guidelines, but at least we did not have to pay a bank interest to borrow our own money! Nor did we have to impact relationships by becoming upset or having to beg for help. That was a blessing.

The first few months were spent being introduced and following up with people and business contacts from Tom. Tom was the business owner/HR specialist that assisted me in trying to find a job after I resigned at MasterCard. Anyway, the verbal agreement we had was that for any business acquired from his introductions, I would pay him 10 percent of the gross receipts for a period of one year from the start of that contract. Since we had nothing, and I had been too absorbed with MasterCard to have entrepreneurial business contacts, that 10 percent certainly seemed reasonable. After all, zero percent of zero is nothing so 10 percent of something was certainly fair. A lot of introductions ensued, but there was no business generated for the first six months.

One day, I received a call asking if I had any consultants with certain skills. Of course, I answered

Believe it or not, she had the exact skills required! God was at work!

yes! A day later, I received an email from someone at MasterCard that I had never met who had heard that I had started an IT consulting firm. He attached a resume of a friend looking for a position.

I forwarded the resume to the potential client, and they agreed that she was a fit. She was our first employee and remained with the company until after the transition to the 100 percent employee owned company (ESOP).

At the time we hired our first employee, we had not incorporated. We immediately contacted the father of our daughter's grade school friend who was a business attorney to assist us. He completed the incorporation process within one day, we submitted the documentation to state and federal agencies, and we were off.

He indicated that equal ownership was often the downfall of small business endeavors. He noted that in the beginning everyone was cooperative and agreeable, but later as challenges arose or extensive growth occurred, disagreements ensued and the break up began.

One key piece of important advice received from that attorney family friend: Do not make the business an even 50 percent business ownership. Someone has to be the tie-breaker and both must agree in the beginning, that person had the final decision.

This was very messy indeed. It was important that co-owners and partners agree at the beginning that at least one person would have majority ownership. It was also important that they agree to abide by the decisions of that person. As a result, Maurice agreed that it would be me with the 51 percent ownership since I was the primary person starting and managing the business. We had determined for financial stability that Maurice would keep his job until such time that the business grew and needed the oversight of both of us.

Some people assumed that we established the business as woman-owned to take advantage of the various industry and government programs available. However, we did not even know at that time that those programs existed. It was simply at the advice of an attorney and his insight concerning the success of businesses when there is at least one owner with the agreed upon authority to make the final decisions. We were learning from the mistakes of others. Since I had no other employment and the time to concentrate on the business, 51 percent ownership logically fell to me. It was several years later that we realized there was some advantage, though small, for being a woman-owned business.

Both of our parents had stressed the importance of working harder and longer. That also equates to doing all that is required. I call it dotting all the "i's" and crossing all of the "t's." (Which is more extensive than "checking all the boxes,") So far, from a business prospective, the "i's" and "t's" that we found important for us to have achieved were:

- Undergraduate and graduate business degrees
- Service to the country as an awarded Air Force Veteran
- Over thirty-five years direct technology and business experience
- Adjunct professor for Washington University in St. Louis teaching undergraduate Operating systems and network communications courses
- Experience managing a major corporation profit and loss business unit
- Experience living internationally
- Functional in a foreign language
- International business experience
- Excellent credit rating
- No outstanding debt (even our cars were paid off)
- Excellent reputation
- Solid community citizen
- Board member with over eight regional non-profit organizations
- Sunday school teacher

All of that was not enough for a very small business loan or for ease of acquiring business clients based on demonstrated technical expertise. There are always choices and solutions. It was important not to let the bank stand in the way of moving forward.

It was also important to remain calm and professional with all the bank personnel as well as business contacts for two reasons:

1) It is important to treat people well (with love) which is biblical, i.e. love your neighbor and do unto others as you would have them do unto you.

2) They might be helpful later and when people know they have not treated you "fairly" they may try to make up for that fact by providing some form of "favor" later.

> **Another wonderful outcome of not obtaining the loan at startup was we built the business with the mindset of no debt. We also continued to manage it without debt. We continued to pay off any line of credit immediately so that we always knew the financials were solid.**

That was extremely important in easing the business stress and later ensured we were able to make business decisions based on what was right rather than being so financially desperate that we would do anything—even something unethically or that stretched the bounds of integrity.

Starting a business was not easy at all. There were constant challenges and difficulties. Fortunately, we were not going after wealth or prestige when we started the business. Circumstances led us to start the business and my strong belief was that I was working for something greater than myself. For example, when we were able to hire someone it was not just about the business, I considered it an honor and responsibility. They were able to feed, clothe, and provide shelter and education for their family.

I remember when we finally reached 100 employees, there was excitement in the office. Someone looked over at the expression on my face and asked what was wrong. I had become "pale" at the thought of being responsible for so many lives. You see, 100 employees meant that we were really responsible for about 300 lives. This is because every employee on the average had at least one spouse and child. Some more and a few unmarried but it was an average. That meant a potential responsibility for three lives with each added employee!

On-the-Job Training Continues

We had our first client and our first employee. I was advised by "experienced" business owners to make the first hires "1099's" which is a class of consultant that does not get benefits. This also made them responsible for their own taxes, both state and federal. Since these business owners had over twenty years of experience classifying their team as 1099's, I followed their advice without too much research. That first client had another requirement a few weeks later and I brought on another 1099 employee. As required, I filed the appropriate forms and tax documents with the state and federal government.

Within the month, I received notice from the state that questioned the status of those individuals. After thorough review, I discovered that it was not appropriate to hire these individuals as 1099's even though others had done so for decades without question. For this class of consultants, they had to actually operate as a business much like a sole proprietor plumber or electrician that you hire to do specific work, but did not direct their work on a day-to-day basis. These individuals were different in that they were hired by me to work at the day-to-day direction of the client. They did not have separate business phones, business cards, and did not have their own insurance. Needless to say, I immediately corrected this and converted them to employees for which we issued a W-2, provided workmen's compensation, and provided health benefits.

> **It was as if God was setting the business and my activity within it on the straight and narrow from the very beginning. This was one time the advice from others was not wise or sound. I should have done more research myself. Lesson learned. Learn from others but always verify!**

Everything was done according to what was required. I realized it was necessary to question and research any advice provided to ensure it was legal, moral, and ethical. I knew and was reminded from the very beginning that it was important to follow the letter as well as the spirit of any and all laws.

When looking for health insurance for them, I found it quite expensive but knew it was a differentiator. It was important if we were to be able to hire good people. We were told that when a company gets to fifty employees, it would be less expensive. However, when we reached fifty it was not less at all. When I inquired why, I was told that when a company reached 100 employees it would be less expensive. It was not. Again I inquired and was informed that at 150 employees, it would be less. It was not. Each time the next level was reached, it seemed that the "bar" was raised.

The road was never easy because I not only had to manage the normal business challenges, but I continually had to deal with being a African American female within the business environment in which there were few. I was quite shocked many times at some of the business practices that were reflective of a certain degree of institutionalized racism. It was somewhat covert and perhaps those involved did not even realize their actions as being racist because it was so prevalent as a norm within some organizations. Several specific instances stand out in my mind.

In 1996 when we first started the business, potential St. Louis clients did not know our company was minority-owned because quite a bit of business was done over the telephone. I was often instructed by either human resources or the potential hiring manager not to send any resumes from specific zip codes that happened to be majority African American communities. The challenge for me was that I knew this was totally wrong yet having just started a business, I did not want to become a martyr and report them. Besides, I did not record the conversation, could not prove they had done this, and would have had to set up a situation in which I could prove they provided these specific instructions. I must point out that if one simply looks at the makeup of the employee base of major corporations they can definitely see the results of this practice. There are very few African American in key positions and far too many departments as well as divisions with no African American representation at all.

I was often referred to the diversity director of corporations and found that it appeared as if the goal was to find reasons not to work with minority companies by filtering them out. One CIO actually told me he was only meeting with me because of the "woman and minority thing" and because the president of the St. Louis Minority Business Council had recommended me. He indicated that he really had no intentions of using our company. He went on to make it clear that he would only be working with IBM or EDS. As often was the case, the conversation was not recorded or witnessed by anyone else.

If I sent in diverse candidates to fill consulting or permanent positions, human resources and the hiring managers often indicated the candidate had great education and skills but did not quite "fit the team." In candid conversations with associates, I learned that it was a way to eliminate African American or minority candidates without experiencing legal problems. I witnessed so many instances in which less qualified non-minorities were hired over African Americans and women as well. There was little I could do. After all, it was and is hard to question "fit" since team work is such a critical factor in the work force.

Unfortunately, these practices served to make minorities actually believe they are not qualified or not good enough. I saw it impacting the self-esteem and their ability to obtain employment in the information technology field in particular. It hurt to see this and experience the racism myself. Needless to say, I did not do business with firms that had these established practices.

As an entrepreneur and as one who believed this was the path God had set me on, I had to continue towards goals in spite of these roadblocks. I could not assist others by getting discouraged and shutting down. Each person that we were able to hire and assign to a client regardless of their race or ethnicity was a movement forward. As we built business credibility, we were able to provide opportunity to many African Americans, other minorities, and women based on their qualifications.

We found that we were constantly battling the tendency of those in charge of hiring vendors for services to look for ways to filter us out rather than understanding the value we added to their company. One potential client was a financial institution. When seeking opportunities with them, the CIO indicated that if they used any of our team for projects they would need background checks and fingerprinting. This was after we had already presented the fact that we performed background checks on all personnel and also many of our team had DOD security clearances, facts he obviously had ignored. He then went on to explain that they were moving much of their applications development and help desk services to India, Pakistan, and China.

When I asked who was handling the background checks and fingerprinting there, he said that he assumed that the vendors they worked with were taking care of that. The background checks and fingerprinting done in those countries were definitely not as extensive as those we were able to conduct. It was also perplexing as to why he would ensure we were specifically aware of the requirements for background checks and fingerprinting (as if we were unable to fulfill the requirement) yet simply assume the vendors he worked with offshore were handling those aspects of security. Of course, we never did any business with that financial institution and not surprising to us, they did later experience severe system security breaches impacting a very large number of their customers.

We were constantly encountering the need to achieve more, dot another "i" or cross another "t." As we examined other vendors and their qualifications, it was obvious we were being held to a different "standard." At first we were too small. The potential clients informed me that when we reached fifty employees they could consider working with our company. We reached fifty employees. They then indicated that we needed to be larger still with at least 100 employees. We also had the added requirement of being in business at least five years. The requirements changed and the "bar" continually rose. Believe it or not, when revenue reached $10 million a few clients indicated that we were a bit too large, and they wanted to give smaller businesses an opportunity! I was actually asked, "Isn't your business big enough?"

I was finally also hit with the requirement to become certified as a minority business. Then I had to become certified as woman-owned. Even after growing to over thirty employees and over $2 million in revenue, I could never seem to get more than 1-2 percent of business from any St. Louis company. In fact even after reaching over 120 employees and $15 million in revenue, and immersing myself in the community through serving and supporting local non-profits, we still never had more than 2 percent of our business within the St. Louis region.

It was obvious even in the first two years of business, I would need to look outside of the region in order to grow the business. As a result, I sought work with the Federal Government.

Working with the Federal Government

I received the notice about a local SBA conference for small businesses and attended as my start into serious work with the federal government. Not knowing anyone there, I sat at a table next to a gentleman, Skip, who was a retired Navy veteran. After we had listened to the presentation and were preparing to leave, he leaned over and inquired about why I was there and asked about my business.

After listening patiently, he leaned over and said, "So you want to do work with the federal government do you, hon?"

Of course I answered, "Yes."

I took no offense to the "hon" in his question because I knew from my time in the Air Force, he was not using it in a negative context but as an endearment much as he would his daughter. He then went on to explain that it took him twelve months to obtain business from a client after a first meeting and that was only if he stayed involved with the client nurturing the relationship. He went on to explain that he was white and connected and since I was a black female, it would be much more difficult. He warned me that it would take 18-24 months to accomplish the same thing, not only because of my race and gender, but also because a female in technology was very rare. Potential clients may not believe I was really the owner of the company.

The expression on my face must have revealed my concern because he then shared that he was not saying those things to discourage me, but to ensure that I realized how difficult it would be and not give up just before a business opportunity was about to unfold. He stressed the importance of nurturing the relationship for two years or more so the client would accept and know me and our business better. I must admit he was exactly right. Practically every opportunity took 18-24 months of constant contact and nurturing of potential clients. The company he worked for would become our first client in the government sector later that year when they awarded us a subcontract with them for work with the federal government.

Like everything else, it was a challenge. That contract required I learn a new system and then hire a small team to deploy and work with that system at various sites within the United States. I would drive over an hour to their offices to begin the training at 7:30 a.m. After spending the day there, I would go to our home office and work; calling potential clients, following up on resumes and possible employees, writing proposals, and preparing for teaching. At that time, I was still teaching at the university two nights a week. My days started at 4 or 4:30 a.m. with prayer, working out, preparing breakfast, showering, and getting dressed for the day. Most often my day did not end until the wee hours of the morning.

As I went forward seeking opportunity in the federal government space, what I found were more "i's to dot and "t's to cross." First, it was important to certify as a federal government minority owned 8(a). This required mounds of paperwork and months to complete. However, it meant that bidding on requests for proposals were limited to only 8(a) certified firms which somewhat reduced the competition. Then woman-owned status required more certification and more paperwork to complete.

We also needed a General Services Administration Schedule (GSA) schedule so there was a contract "vehicle" from which agencies could order requiring yet more documentation and coordination with people in Washington, DC. After a few months of submitting our documentation and receiving changes to make from the contracting officer in order to receive the GSA schedule, I set up an appointment, got on a plane to DC with all previous requested changes completed, and a laptop so I had the ability to change things on the spot. Good thing, too. There were, of course, more changes. I questioned one requested change because after reviewing the GSA schedules of other firms, I noticed they did not incorporate the changes being requested of me.

The Contracting Officer abruptly said, "That is their GSA schedule. You are trying to get yours. Do you want it or not?"

My immediate reply was, "Yes ma'am! What was that change again?"

I made the change and left DC with our GSA schedule in hand. Of course, it was only a contract vehicle which basically means you have the ability to market to agencies that might have opportunity and need of your services. Agencies often only had to select three companies with applicable GSA schedules to bid on their requirement. Other times it was full and open which meant any of the millions of businesses with applicable skills were able to submit bids to the request for proposal. Bottom line, it was mandatory to have, but like 8(a) status, it in no way guaranteed any business opportunity. It was a "fishing license" of sorts and a way to possibly get on the list of bidders.

Then we were informed by our business developer, who had experience as a government Contracting Officer, that each agency had their own contract vehicles. So we proceeded to determine and apply for several contract schedules with agencies that used IT and cyber-security services. We found that a security clearance was a great differentiator so we proceeded to obtain that, too! I often joke about the fact that to receive the top secret clearance one had to undergo all kinds of investigations, stopping just short of a colonoscopy.

Now there were some agencies that said everything we had was good, but if we were certified as Veteran-owned they would do business with us. Then other agencies indicated, if only we were a disabled veteran-owned that would change the playing field. Since both of us served in the Air Force, that was simply a matter of providing the DD-214. As for disabled-veteran owned, I had surgery while in the Air Force that caused impairment of my left index finger. Also, I had the start of bunions on my feet before going into the Air Force, but they worsened while on active duty and were documented in my medical records before my honorable discharge.

I proceeded to obtain disabled veteran status because it required at least 10 percent or more disability. For some reason, the doctor at the VA hospital allowed 10 percent for the finger, but nothing for my more impactful bunions. He stated a concern that since the bunions caused some pain and my toes were obviously impaired, I would probably request surgery that would have to be covered. Either way, he did not provide any assistance as it related to the bunions and I did not protest the decision. The mission to obtain the requested disabled veteran status was accomplished. I disregarded my own needs (the bunions) because I did not have time to worry about correcting the situation with my bunions. It was about the business growth for stability so people could remain employed and/or have career growth opportunities.

So in summary, the "i's" and "t's" list now included:
- Undergraduate and graduate business degrees
- Service to the country as an Air Force Veteran
- Over thirty-five years direct technology and business experience
- Adjunct professor for Washington University in St. Louis teaching undergraduate Operating systems and network communications courses
- Experience managing a major corporation profit and loss business unit
- Experience living internationally
- Functional in a foreign language
- International business experience
- Excellent credit rating

- No outstanding debt (even our cars were paid off)
- Excellent reputation
- Solid community citizen
- Board member with over eight regional non-profit organizations
- Sunday school teacher
- Certified as minority-owned
- Certified as 8(a)
- Certified as woman-owned
- GSA schedule
- Contract vehicles from over five government agencies
- Top Secret Security Clearance (Individual -both Maurice and I and corporate)
- Veteran-Owned
- Disabled Veteran-Owned

*2009 Girl Scouts Woman of Distinction

*2007 Webster University *School of Business Alumni of the Year

*2007Distinguished Entrepreneur Award (Dr. Martin Luther King, Jr. State Celebration Commission of MO)

*2006 IT Firm of the Year Midwest Region (MED – Chicago)

*2006 One of 25 Most Influential Business Women

*2006 Scott AFB Chapter AFCEAN of the Year

*2006 Athena Leadership Foundation Award

*Deloitte Touché Regional Technology Fast 50 (3rd in 2001, 11th in 2002, 2nd in 2003, Regional Top 50 list in 2004, 2005, 2006)

*Deloitte Touché National Technology Fast 500 (ranked 175th in 2001, 210th in 2003, 144th in 2004, 225th in 2005, & 375th in 2006)

*INC 500 America's Fastest Growing Private Business (ranked 269 in 2004, 275 in 2005)

*INC 500/5000 America's Fastest Growing Private Business (ranked 4,533 in 2006)

*2005 SBA Missouri Small Business Person of the Year

*2005 YWCA Special Leadership Awardee

*2005 Missouri Chamber of Commerce Industry Fast Track

*2004 Entrepreneur of the Year – St. Louis American and RCGA

*2004 Tri-County Entrepreneur of the Year – Technology Sector

*2003 Professional Organization of Women Top Ten African American Woman of Distinction

*2003 NAWBO Distinguished Woman Business Owner of the Year

*2003 USDA OPPM Woman-Owned Business of the Year

*2003 NMSDC Regional Supplier of the Year

*2002 Missouri Small Business of the Year (Governor's Award)

*2002 USDA Rural Development Woman-Owned Business of the Year

*2002 & 2000 St. Louis Minority Business Council Minority Business Enterprise of the Year

Maurice & Brenda Receiving the NMSDC Award

I knew from discussions and meetings with them that my competitors had not had the same hoops to jump through before obtaining business in the commercial or government "world," even some much larger firms did not. The bottom line is that rather than getting upset and being a victim, whenever a client indicated that they would do business with me if we had a certain criteria or status, if applicable and legal, I would proceed to take the time and effort to obtain it.

Eventually, there was nothing else to request or require. The solid foundation had been acquired. In spite of all of the "i's" dotted and "t's" crossed and all of the dedication and commitment within the region through work with non-profit organizations, the fact remained that less than 2 percent of our business was ever with companies within the St. Louis region.

But God...

However, what God has planned for us cannot be determined by humankind. We had some fantastic people on our team that were extremely instrumental in moving the business forward.

I chose not to name them, their functions or the value they added at the risk of missing someone that added tremendous value. However, I can say that even when someone was difficult or felt they had to quit and move on or even if they were fired or laid off, they were important for company growth and fit the purpose that God had for them and the company at that place and time. So I must state that if anyone tells you that they worked for the Newberry Group, Inc. you can be sure they are quality people and added value. I am in no way implying that everyone was an angel or that they were perfect because many people actually created challenges, tried to create dysfunction or were difficult to work with and created problems that we had to resolve. However, for the most part, in each case and in retrospect, I understand why God brought them into our lives and company when He did.

Some knew financials and others knew government regulations. Some were great technically and administratively while others knew contracting and proposals. The company grew to over $19 million in revenue with business in many states and internationally as well. Some of the business was commercial and quite a bit was government.

It was never easy and required many hours of dedicated work. All client and employee business or related work had to be done during "normal" business hours. This meant that the early proposals I had to personally complete because we did not have any corporate overhead type of employees. This had to be done after hours into the wee hours of the morning. Even after we grew, Maurice and I were most often the last ones out of the office, leaving as late as 10 or 11:00 p.m. most evenings. Fortunately by then we were "empty nesters."

It was a difficult and challenging journey. However, as you can see, being born African American and female allowed for the various certifications: having a strong family structure allowed for lessons on character, commitment, integrity, and morals; having served in the Air Force allowed us to be veterans and taught us about perseverance, determination, and mission focus. Having the surgery on my finger allowed for disability status; and having worked at MasterCard and the sweatshop type environment prepared me to do what it takes to run a business, market, and establish a solid brand. Teaching IT courses at Washington University also added to my credibility. It truly did all come together for good. Here's what one journalist reported,

Through it all, she [Newberry] kept a consistent, positive movement despite any roadblocks she experienced due to her race or gender. "Denying the issues does not help," she says. "However, it does hurt to allow oneself to become a victim or paralyzed from the challenges. After all, we are all working for something greater than ourselves and to not appreciate your blessings and do your very best is an insult to the greater good."(St. Louis Small Business Monthly, August 2011)

Building a business is much more about others and leaving a legacy. The landscape of business is littered with self-centered business enterprises that come and go making a few wealthy, but enriching the lives of only a very few. What would our legacy be?

Nuggets for Living Fully and Successfully

Below is the list of "i's" we had to dot and "t's" we had to cross in order to achieve our business goals. Check off the ones you are already using and circle the ones you may need to begin to implement or complete in your own life. Some of them may not relate to you or your goals and background. For instance, you may not desire to join the military or perhaps you may exceed the age limitation. Think of any service that may be applicable to you such as the Peace Corp, Teach-for-America, serving as a volunteer or serving on the board of non-profit organizations, volunteering at your work, in your community or church. Perhaps you are unable to be an adjunct professor, but you may be able to mentor young people in your area of expertise. Add others that may relate to your specific situation and move toward achieving them.

- Undergraduate and graduate business degrees
- Service to the country as an Air Force Veteran
- Over thirty-five years direct technology and business experience
- Adjunct professor for Washington University in St. Louis teaching undergraduate Operating systems and network communications courses
- Experience managing a major corporation profit and loss business unit
- International business experience
- Excellent credit rating
- No outstanding debt (even our cars were paid off)
- Excellent reputation
- Solid community citizen
- Board member with over eight regional non-profit organizations
- Sunday school teacher
- Certified as minority-owned
- Certified as 8(a)
- Certified as woman-owned
- GSA schedule

- Contract vehicles from over five government agencies
- Top Secret Security Clearance (Individual and corporate)
- Veteran-Owned
- Disabled Veteran-Owned
- Other: _____

Everything was done according to what was required. I realized it was necessary to question and research any advice provided to ensure it was legal, morale, and ethical. I knew and was reminded from the very beginning that it was important to follow the letter as well as the spirit of any and all laws.

List the advantages of ensuring you follow the letter as well as spirit of the law in business:

_____

_____

_____

_____

The Weight of Legacy (St. Louis Business Monthly/August 2011 by Jeremy Nulik)

"Newberry's discipline is difficult to match, but she has a partner in business and life in her husband, Maurice, who joined her at The Newberry Group, a technology company that she founded in 1996. Together they would wake up at 4 a.m. to have discussions about the business as they walked or jogged around their neighborhood. Their tireless pursuit has paid off; having achieved a legacy, having created a better life for her children, having made good on the responsibility she feels she has as an African American woman, having acted on the faith that defines her life, and she has done it all before retirement age. What legacy do you hope to achieve with your business or endeavors?"

Chapter 7

THE WEIGHT OF LEGACY

Good people leave an inheritance to their grandchildren.

(Proverbs 13:22 NLT)

U nfortunately, when many people spout off about balance, what I have found upon further conversations is that what many really want are all the perks and a large income, but to receive them with less work. However, I have found that premise simply defies natural law. If a farmer sows twenty acres of land to feed his family for a year and then decides the next year he wants more balance in life so he sows only ten acres, his family definitely will not be fed equally that year in which he sows less and perhaps will only eat half of that year.

Likewise a company cannot reward part-time workers with the same career opportunities, financial provisions, and promotions that they give to full-time workers. How fair would that be? Additionally, if one is more productive and supports the company and team better than others, it would stand to reason that person would obtain more financial provisions, career opportunities, and promotions than those that are not productive or "team players."

Bottom line, everyone must make decisions and live with the consequences whether good, bad or difficult. No one is to blame if you decide to take several years to work less or decide to drop out of school. Each of those decisions have long term and possibly damaging effects on a life. However, no one is to blame for those decisions or their ramifications but the one that makes them.

There is absolutely nothing wrong with taking months or years off from working on your career. However, know that there will be consequences and perhaps, from a career perspective, you may not "catch up." If that decision creates less stress or is important for your family or education attainment, then you may gain in so many other ways. Only you can determine your path and what works best for you. When you are at peace with your decisions, you are not a victim and you are better able to contribute to society as a whole in the way that best suits you and your purpose.

Therefore, it is important to sow a lot of good works, words, emotions, and actions. Make solid decisions based on your goals and dreams. Create a foundation and work to continue building upon it. If you decide to take a pause and reduce your load, realize that it will impact your future so be willing to accept the consequences whether good or bad. It is a natural law. Sow abundantly. Reap abundantly. Sow less. Reap less.

> **Remember, "If you sow in the wind you will reap in the whirlwind — both good and bad."**

Life balance ebbs and flows. Some weeks or years will be slower, maybe only because the company makes changes or your kids have fewer activities. But in those slower times, embrace it and use the time wisely. The important thing is to keep moving forward. Do not stop.

Walt Disney is quoted as saying, "Around here we don't look backwards for very long. We keep moving forward, opening up new doors, and doing new things because we are curious and curiosity keeps leading us down new paths."

Learning Balance

During my own career building days and work years, while I often worked sixteen to twenty-hour days, it never occurred to me to concentrate on balance. Ensuring I was a valuable resource for my bosses and approaching work in doing what God intended was the focus. I wanted to keep my job and not be laid off or fired. However, it was important to me that Maurice and I work together to ensure our girls knew they were loved and safe. We felt that it was essential that they have adequate food, decent shelter, and a great education so that they would have a solid foundation to be wonderful independent adults that could have rewarding careers and be of value to society just as my parents had done for me only better.

We wanted them to have choices in life. If that meant they wanted to be a stay-at-home mother because they did not have student loans, had savings and supportive husbands, great. If they wanted careers, then great. Bottom line is that we wanted to provide them with solid foundations without financial or other burdens. After all aren't we responsible for ensuring each generation was better that the previous? Well, we thought so and heard our parents and grandparents express that as a responsibility. If not ensuring each generation is better, then at least ensuring they have the foundation to do better if they desire. Aren't we called to leave a legacy for our children and our children's children (Proverbs 13:22)? Many today may not buy into that mindset, but that is the mindset that gave us the motivation and goals to excel for our own family as well as those of our business teams.

There were times when Maurice, who worked in applications programming at a different company, and I were on call at the same time. We would discuss who would be done first, rouse up our daughters who were sleeping and take them along. Often times I would make them a little sleeping area under my desk like a camp out. At the time and their ages, they seemed to enjoy the experience. We knew it was not an easy decision as it disrupted plans for that day or the next and often caused them to lose some sleep. But without family in the region and solid remote access at the time, it was part of the requirements of the job. If one did not accept being on call for system emergencies then one would need to seek a different career because being on call and responding was a normal expectation for technology staff at most companies during those days. Fortunately, the times I remember this happening were in the summer and before our daughters were in school so we did not cause any risks to their performance at school.

To ensure proper nutrition for our family since work was often a bit erratic, I would create our menu and grocery list on Wednesday, Maurice would shop for groceries on Thursdays taking the girls along, and I would cook in bulk for the following week on either Saturday or Sunday depending on which day time allowed. While I cooked, I watched, talked to or played with the girls, and Maurice did yard work. Often they would play outside while Maurice did the yard work. That was the routine we were able to work out to bring balance when our lives got hectic. The leftovers from Sundays became dinner on Tuesday. The leftovers from the Monday dinner I had prepared on the weekend would become the Wednesday dinner. Thursday while grocery shopping, the girls selected a frozen dinner treat from our approved list, of course.

Thursday evening one or both of us cleaned house to free up the weekend. Friday night was our "date night," but we spent it at home. The girls could pick out fast food, one of us would begin washing clothes so they would all be done by Saturday. Maurice would cook our seafood dinner while I read and tucked the girls into bed and then we would eat together while watching a favorite TV show. Saturdays we would rise early, Maurice or I would iron all ten white catholic school blouses and the pleated skirts for the week.

In the summers when the girls were young without their sport activities, I would prepare their breakfast and a picnic lunch to take to the park while Maurice did yard work.

Sometimes there was time to do the prep work for cooking the dinners. We would then get dressed and drive to Forest Park with bikes in tow. We would ride around the bike paths several times, stop in at the zoo to see a few animals, then ride to one of the lakes where we ate lunch and fed the ducks. These were really fun family times! We worked hard and set aside time to enjoy each other as a family. Then it was back home, baths and showers followed by family movie night with pizza as a treat. Early on it was a frozen pizza that we "improved upon" with extra cheese and meat. Later as our salaries improved we were able to get pizza delivered.

Sundays were also family days where we played together, and when they were younger we went to church. Then I did the bulk of the cooking for the week. That was also the day we all prepped for the week putting up clothes that had been washed and ironed, doing homework, watching sports, and resting. Once we were able to afford it, we installed an in-ground pool. We would spend summer Saturdays and Sundays in the pool rather than on bikes in Forest Park.

Each weekday morning I would get up, read scripture, pray, and then we would work out by either jogging or using tapped exercise programs. I would prepare breakfast for the girls ensuring each morning was different. Home-made pancakes, oatmeal, cream of wheat, eggs with sausage, biscuits with Canadian bacon and egg, English muffins or toast with instant breakfast are some examples. Very seldom would they have cold cereal. I never felt it was filling enough. I prepared lunch each day, got myself ready for work, and would drive them to school. If I was traveling on business, Maurice took on the morning tasks of preparing the girls for school.

As you can tell, there was little time for thinking about balance. There was only time to do the best that we could in every facet of life. It was a lot to do, but we knew our responsibilities and our goals. Our children were of prime importance even though work took tremendous time and effort. We knew, however, without work, there was not an opportunity to provide healthy food, decent shelter, clothing, and the best education possible for our girls.

We worked as partners to take care of the home, manage the girls and their activities, and prepare a healthy environment. It was a partnership and we did not dwell on whether the household work was equal, we just kept our focus on our goals for the children and did what worked at the phase of life we were in. So, while it felt extremely busy with no time to really relax or truly socialize with friends, it was our way of seeking the balance required to get everything done on the journey towards our goals.

God had entrusted us with wonderful, healthy, intelligent, and beautiful children. It was our responsibility to get them successfully into adulthood with as few "childhood scars" as possible.

Discipline, Commitment, and Sacrifice

For the moment, all discipline seems painful rather than pleasant, but layer it yields the peaceful fruit of righteousness to those who have been trained by it. (Hebrews 12:11)

People have often asked about how I achieved various accomplishments and in retrospect, besides a constant faith in the Lord, the blessed love of my life partner, and unconditional family love with strong values and positive influence, it comes down to discipline, commitment, and sacrifice.

Due to the desire to maintain employment and do my best, I found that I could not control the end of my work day. So in order to get exercise in, the mornings were my best option. Even when pregnant, I would awake every morning and walk at 5:30 a.m. with a wonderful neighbor who had a new baby and was awake anyway. She was encouragement for me and I am sure I was for her as well. We loved our morning talks.

There were times early in my career I was able to get off at the same time each day due to carpooling. Maurice carpooled also. This allowed us to work out together in the evenings instead of early mornings. The point is that exercise for health became and remains a lifelong commitment that required changes in time or method as life changed. With each change a commitment to the new schedule was also required.

Another area was nutrition. I was committed to ensuring my family had a special most important meal of the day. I loved them and wanted to send them off prepared and ready. One bonus that I discovered is that breakfasts prepared are cheaper than cold cereal and most often contained better nourishment. I would "spike" their homemade pancakes with wheat germ, add apples and cinnamon to their oatmeal, make cream of wheat with milk, make them egg muffins with Canadian bacon, added wheat germ and blueberries or apples to fully homemade muffins, and periodically allow frozen Apple strudel teamed with an instant breakfast drink. I varied the breakfasts so they would not get bored and made "from scratch" many of the variations of muffins and pancakes because that way I knew what they contained.

It took discipline to ensure the shopping list and pantry had the necessary items for these breakfasts. I also made menus each week from which the shopping list was created. This ensured we had healthy meals. Of course we allowed treats of fast food or a frozen meal once or twice a week so the girls did not feel deprived and had that experience, but most days they had what I had cooked either that day or as leftovers.

We valued education so we drove our children to and from their private Catholic school. It was a sacrifice and required discipline to ensure they completed all of their school work. This provided our girls the discipline for their own life endeavors. They each received college academic scholarships. Our oldest received a "full ride" which was critical because I had no salary at that time since we had just started the business.

Teaching evening undergraduate and graduate operating system and network communications courses at Washington University in St. Louis once or twice per week for over twenty years was not easy either. There was preparation required for the class lectures, exams, and I needed to consistently be reliable to teach. This was in addition to having a career and family. It required preparation on the weekends and some evenings. It was not easy, but it kept me sharp in my knowledge of technology as students offered challenges. It also provided additional credibility with clients. It was a small yet effective differentiator in the business marketplace.

Traveling for business was interesting as well as a challenge. It was often lonely, but it was what was required for my position. The greater the position, the greater the responsibility and expectations. I was blessed with travel to Bogota, Columbia, Caracas, Venezuela, Santiago, Chile, but those trips required great time away from family. However, Maurice was supportive and our family unit remained intact because we were in concert about family long-term goals. Maurice never resented this nor made me feel guilty.

Once we started the business, new orders of discipline were required. If I was a non-profit Board member, I ensured that I participated in committees and supported the organization with the time, talent, and treasures available to me at the time. Often this meant driving thirty miles for 7:30 a.m. meetings, driving back to the office, only to repeat the trip for evening meetings or events. This helped with networking, brand development, and provided an introduction of our business to potential clients. The goal was to grow the company to secure projects, grow the business, and thus obtain increased job security and employment opportunities for our team, but it required a new level of discipline, commitment, and sacrifice.

I often hear people starting a business without thinking it through and considering the discipline, commitment, and sacrifice that will be required. One must be prepared to do all tasks required. Ever had to change printer toner cartridge at your corporate job? Ever had to learn a new skill without a formal class? Ever prepared your own proposals start to finish after a full day of client meetings or work? Ever had to create and follow a business budget? Ever had to consistently work 16-20 hour days for years? Ever had to put your house up for collateral for your business risking the roof over your head and the future financial stability of your family? Ever had to pay taxes on money you did not get paid, but kept in the business for stability and payroll? Ever go two or more years without pay so the company survived? Ever had to pay others while you went without a paycheck? Ever had to take care of, clean the office and empty the office trash every day because you needed to preserve cash? Ever take over a 50 percent cut in pay after an economic crisis so you could retain staff? Well, as an early, mid and sometimes late stage entrepreneur, you just might do any and all of these and more. I did. We did.

Because of some early decisions such as the goal and achievement of paying off our house in about sixteen years, the commitment to eliminate debt, establish a solid foundation for our girls so they received academic scholarships, drive vehicles for twelve years or more, and staying committed to each other and our marriage, we had the foundation to allow such discipline, commitment, and sacrifice required to own our business.

Sometimes when life was hectic and I found myself feeling sorry for myself, I would stop and thank God for the strength, ability, and opportunities He had afforded me.

Little did I realize the discipline, commitment, and sacrifice that was always so much a part of my life would become even more important when I was diagnosed and treated for stage IV tongue cancer. It was and is important to build the immune system to allow normal cells to prevail and reduce the stress on the entire system. Through research and as a result of unofficial advice from oncologists and radiologists, I began and continue on a plant-based diet. This means very little to no animal protein, no dairy, no "bad" fats, and a host of recommended supplements to assist in rebuilding the "good" cells and helping the immune system eliminate the normal toxins as well as the toxins that remained after chemo and radiation. Not easy. It required and continues to require a whole new relationship with food.

Of course one could say, with all the discipline, commitment and sacrifice, I was still subjected to cancer. I submit to you that my treatment and healing results thus far were better because of the condition of my health and body. Bottom line is that without discipline, commitment and sacrifice, it is quite impossible to accomplish many if not most things in life. Make no mistake, shortcuts are the exception and often lead to a shaky foundation full of doubt, depression, guilt, and the like. Taking the "road less traveled" of discipline, commitment, and sacrifice most often will create a solid foundation that, over time, leads to peace, material blessings, and joy that surpasses all understanding.

Sure sometimes one must make changes as you grow, accomplish interim goals and other areas of your life itself changes, but it is important to design new routines and disciplines to successfully complete the key elements for that time in your life. It is important to be flexible while also fulfilling the necessary components to achieve your goals and dreams. Time for God, time with family, your career, your health, and your finances requires balance, discipline, commitment, and sacrifice, but they are all worth it in the long run!

The Weight of Legacy

Neither of our girls were interested in owning and running the company. We knew we would not live or be extremely healthy forever and creating stability for the employees was important. Based on that we planned for the future of our employees and transitioned the company to 100 percent employee-opened (ESOP) in March 2008. The greatest economic downturn since the Great Depression occurred in September 2008. The transition may have either been difficult or impossible had it not been completed in March. We could never have predicted or planned for that, but God knew and placed the time for the transition in our hearts. God also knew of the health challenge I would be experiencing. Not being the owner of a company while going through surgery, chemo, and radiation was important to my health and recovery. I was able to concentrate on treatment and healing without the stress of owning and running the business. We wanted and needed to provide a path for business survival, growth, and continuation when we were no longer the owners of the company we had birthed.

We researched extensively and deduced that a 100 percent ESOP structure allowed for the employee-owners to have and continue to gain equity in the company without any personal financial investment or risk. It also did not put us in a position of conflicting interests. The employees did not have to personally buy stock. They simply needed to work and as the company grew, it would pay for the "debt shares" and their own equity would grow as well. Equity ownership without any personal financial risk or investment! We thought we were giving them a gift. Business ownership without personal risk or investment was and is quite unusual.

In our research, we read and talked to others that had transitioned to an ESOP and found that employees were extremely pleased at the outcome as well as their company growth when they focused on growing the company. This was because they realize that it was growing their own equity value as well. They only needed to work just as they would at any other company. Many ESOP companies of various sizes, including a great many with over 1000 employees were successful well-known brands. Some were even located in the St. Louis and Kansas City market. We noted companies such as Publix super markets, Black & Veatch, Graybar Electric, Burns & McDonnell Engineering, Applied Research Associates, Bob's Red Mill, McCarthy Building Company, and Sterling Global Operations were successful ESOPs. We talked with many and did everything possible to ensure it was handled the correct way to include hiring the best firms possible to handle all aspects of the transaction based on recommendations from those already transitioned to an ESOP. The process went well and completed in March of 2008.

In January 2009, we hired a new president and CEO whom we thought was highly qualified. He had run a business unit of a major defense contractor with revenues over $800 million and had an extremely skilled background in technology and cyber security. It was just the type of work our company did only much larger. He even had a higher level security clearance than either of us. We felt certain he would be able to take a much smaller company like ours with just under $20 million in revenues to the next level and beyond. We felt this would ensure growth and result in substantial equity for the employees over time. To ensure success and reduce the "looking back at the founders" syndrome that others had reported as a challenge for transitions, we stopped participating in the day-to-day functions in April 2009. That relieved everyone of any ambiguity or stress regarding who was in charge of the business.

Unfortunately, some people did not understand the gift of a 100 percent ESOP and resented the fact that we moved on. They were only concerned or resentful of what we gained without understanding what we had sacrificed for them. We could have just sold the company to an investor or even just shut it down slowly and deliberately keeping all the proceeds and gain. But we chose instead to provide a path to greater financial opportunity for the employees. As they grew the company from where it was they would create wealth for themselves without risking their homes and financial security as we had to do. Our goal was to provide a legacy.

To further demonstrate faith in the transition, the CEO and the company foundation, we agreed to provide the collateral by retaining it in cash with the bank so that if the company had difficulties, there were options for managing the debt to us and the company would not just be seized by the bank. Only the collateral we provided would be seized so the major risk was to us.

Alas, as the work was challenging and difficult mostly due to the economic crisis, 3 years after the ESOP transaction the CEO questioned the independent valuation that was completed in early 2008 for the ESOP. The company ended up just defaulting on the debt. Basically, nothing more was paid to the bank and the bank then seized all of the cash we had provided as collateral. The company continued to function and grow, but for us that meant we ultimately received much less than half of the valuation amount, but paid taxes as if we had received all of the funds. This was quite disappointing and impacted us financially, but we are not angry. We continued to realize that God is our provider and we did not ever put our trust in mankind. We took the risk and accepted the consequences, though we did not anticipate being taken advantage of and receiving less than half of the value that was independently determined by one of the best valuation firms in the industry.

We are firm believers that vengeance is not ours and that those who determined that defaulting on the debt to us was better than working with us to ultimately restructure it and continue to grow the company, would receive their "justice" in whatever manner God deemed appropriate.

As for us, God positioned us for either outcome. Our gift remains as we intended. The future success or not of the company is theirs to determine just as it was ours. We definitely wish to see great growth and equity creation for the employees. After all, that is what legacy is all about. And, how shall we view our successes in life? We often live life seeking to acquire and win the battles ahead of us. Sometimes giving does hurt and can grieve the giver when those in receipt are not appreciative, but we realize we must give without expectations of any kind. What mindset do we need in life's journey? Such is a question we must now explore.

Nuggets for Living Fully and Successfully

Remember, "If you sow in the wind you will reap in the whirlwind—both good and bad."

It is important to sow a lot of good "seed." (Galatians 6:7)

Make solid decisions based on your goals and dreams.

Create a foundation and work to continue building upon it.

If you decide to take a pause and reduce your load, realize that it will impact your future so be willing to accept the consequences.

Sow. Reap. Sow less. Reap less.

Balance Is Important: (Philippians 3:14)

Maurice and I worked as partners to take care of the home, manage the girls and their activities, and prepare a healthy environment. We did not dwell on whether the household work was equal, we just kept our focus on our goals for the children and did what worked at the phase of life we were in.

Create a Legacy: (Proverbs 13:22; Psalm 127:3)

God had entrusted us with wonderful, healthy, intelligent and beautiful children. It was our responsibility to get them successfully into adulthood with as few "childhood scars" as possible. Children are a heritage from God (Psalm 127:3-5)

Discipline, Commitment, and Sacrifice: (Hebrews 12:11)

People have often ask about how I achieved various accomplishments and in retrospect, besides a constant faith in the Lord, the blessed love of my life partner, and unconditional family love with strong values and positive influence, it comes down to *discipline, commitment, and sacrifice.* How is your discipline and commitment? Any sacrifices?

What legacy do you hope to achieve with your career, business, endeavors, and family?

What It Takes (St. Louis Small Business Monthly/ August 2011 by Jeremy Nulik)

Tenacity: "When you hear negative things said, you can't dwell on them," says Newberry. "In the Air Force, you understand that things can be tough, but you do what needs to be done to accomplish the goal as long as it is legal, ethical, and moral. You don't let others define you."

Chapter 8

HAVE OR HAVE NOT

The Hypocrisy

Love is not jealous or boastful or proud or rude.
— St. Paul to the Corinthians[3]

I t seems that no matter the socio-economic status or faith-walk, we are subject to the jealousy of others. Often this jealousy becomes more noticeable as our economic status improves. In thinking about it, it may be because people generally are not envious of the poor and middle class. Therefore, those that have excess material comfort tend to be the target of envy, anger or admiration. I was hit right in the face with this early in the start of our business.

When we first started the business, I was driving an eight-year-old car in extremely great condition. Maurice and I valued the blessings received and he has always kept our vehicles in great condition through keeping them clean inside and out as well as ensuring the required maintenance

---

[3] 1 Corinthians 13:4b (NLT)

was done. This is why we were able to drive that old Fiat Sport Spider convertible in Spain and sell it for the same amount we had paid for it after three and half years of driving it. It was the second car for which that occurred. Our first car was a brand new, yellow Toyota Celica that we bought in Tucson, Arizona. We received our orders to report to the base in Spain which meant we had to sell our car quickly. An Air Force officer wanted a small car for his daughter, and in the early 1970s with the long gas lines due to oil shortages, small cars were in demand. That car sold with no depreciation.

Needless to say, after seeing what car care and maintenance can do for such a generally depreciating asset, I never bothered Maurice about the time he spent cleaning and maintaining our vehicles. It was part of his upbringing. When he was a teen, his father required that he clean the family car inside and out in order to use it for dating. He gained the understanding about how to take care of vehicles especially when it was the only mode of transportation for the whole family. That early lesson never left his psyche.

During that first year of business, it was quite tough because all the money we earned went right back into the business. Only the employees were paid. There was no extra for my paycheck or other frills. I had made arrangements to meet with a potential client of a major corporation to take them to lunch.

When one gentleman got into the car, he looked at it and said, "I guess business is not very good if this is the best car you can drive. How good should I assume your business is doing? Do you even have any clients?"

After pausing I responded, "Well, business is fine, I just chose to reinvest in the business."

He just laughed and said that he hoped that I was not desperate for business or seeking sympathy. This event stuck with me and I realized that frugality was not valued by many people, and the fact that my frugality could actually be perceived negatively, was very surprising to me. By contrast, other people are negative when business owners or sales people drive fancy cars or even have private planes. Or they make the assumption that the business is super successful. In fact driving luxury cars or private planes may be a reflection of a business with major debt. It is interesting how people make assumptions and judgments simply based on a business owner or leader's mode of transportation.

Fast forward several years and our business had grown substantially. Now we were able to lease a great car for business. I remember driving it to a client meeting. I parked the car quite a distance away not wanting to "showcase" the car for fear of just the opposite reaction. By then I had been made aware that some potential clients would not want to provide a business opportunity if they believed you to be doing too well. Their thought would be you do not need more business especially if, from their perception, you were doing better than they were.

These contrasting world views were difficult to work around, but knowing they existed allowed me to come "to the table" better prepared. Understand though, I never personally considered anyone's transportation as a barometer of whether I should provide them a business opportunity or not. So it was quite enlightening when this business meeting gave me yet a still different perspective. Upon exiting the restaurant, I was hesitant to go towards the car thinking that she might be resentful of another's material blessing.

However, she inquired, "Where are you parked? Where is your car?"

I hesitated and pointed to the car with what must have been an uncomfortable body and facial expression because she proceeded to say, "No need to be ashamed or embarrassed with the material blessings from God. He blesses people materially, too. How ironic it would be if only horrible and evil people had material comfort beyond the necessities. If you have abided by the Lord and given Him, your family and your fellow man your time, talents, and treasures there is no reason God would not provide added material comfort. He knows who will have a giving and humble heart so it would be logical that He would provide material blessings knowing they would glorify Him."

After her enlightening comments, we then discussed King David and other Old and New Testament examples of God using the rich as well as poor to achieve His purposes. She eased my concerns about this topic,

> **Do not to be ashamed or embarrassed with the material blessings from God. Praise Him for His provision; do not take personal credit or pride in it.**

at least for a while. As a human with strong faith, I have finally accepted the fact that God creates and allows His people to be conflicted about material comfort and physical blessings. It seems to be by design so that we remain concerned and "in check" about knowing He is in control and glorified when Christians recognize their blessings, tithe, and present offerings by giving to various charities or causes, while they maintain and increase their philanthropy due to their belief and not in an effort to earn their way into heaven. After all, eternal life is a gift of mercy and grace, not because of what one has done.[4]

We are all sinners and have the potential to become prideful or arrogant. That is why the warning is in the Bible about the rich having difficulty getting to heaven and loving money being evil.[5] Those that are rich or materially comfortable way beyond the necessities often have more distractions and temptations. After all, are you aware of beautiful young

---

[4] See Romans 6:23 and Ephesians 2:8

[5] See Matthew 19:23, 1 Timothy 6:10, and 1 Peter 5:2

women flirting with and going after poor un-powerful men? Do those struggling to put food on the table have the distraction of managing their maids, butlers, private plane or boat? The rich and powerful seem to have more temptations and distractions that may impact their time with and for godly purposes, but that does not condemn them to hell if they follow the Lord. It also does not mean they will automatically be morally corrupt or prideful.

Those with material comfort beyond the necessities have more responsibility towards their fellow man. "To whom much is given, much is required" (Luke 12:48).

> **When one knows the Lord, they want to follow Christian principals and neither pride nor arrogance is part of those principals.**

This is biblical and an admired businessman understands this message as well. During a speech at Harvard University in 2007, Bill Gates shared the fact that his mother had used an opportunity to deliver this message by putting these very words into a letter to his wife, Melinda, at her bridal shower. His mother was very ill with cancer at the time, but even then felt the need to stress this truth. As we all know their material blessings are "off the charts," but their actions of philanthropy demonstrate their understanding of the responsibility of "much is required."

Think about it. If everyone gave everything away to others then who would be left to give? The point is to be charitable, ensure God gets at least your first 10 percent, and that offerings and donations are also given.[6] As an additional note, the act of purchasing goods and services also helps because people are hired to provide them and their jobs allow them to also give to God and others while also providing food, shelter, clothing, and education for their family. Therefore, material blessings beyond the

---

[6] See Malachi 3:8-10

necessities allows for helping others through the purchase of additional goods and services. For example, when people buy Starbucks coffee that many believe is a splurge and too expensive, it allows Starbucks to not only create jobs but to also donate to various global causes that assists the poor and to purchase goods from developing countries as well.

As an aside, we did have one of our own business advisory board members ask us, "Isn't your company big enough? Don't you have enough business? Why would you even want more business?"

This was quite strange because business either grows or dies just like anything else from plants to fish to humans. To cease to grow is a journey towards extinction. Additionally, clients may cease doing business and contracts can end at unexpected times so it is imperative that a business continue to seek new opportunities while still taking care of and nurturing current clients. I am still perplexed as to why, when our business grew beyond certain levels, we were told we were large enough or did not "need" more business. Sometimes I thought they only expressed those thoughts because I was a Black female. I have never heard a white male questioned about growing their business. After all, that is what business does when the people work hard.

However, to remove the victim mentality, Maurice and I used those questions as a call to reflection. At each point in growth, different decisions and impacts to personal life were encountered so we learned to build on what we learned and continued to grow in wisdom and experience.

"I want them to recognize us as a growing, global IT consultancy that can help them with their IT," Brenda said in an interview for the St. Louis Woman's Magazine (March 2007).

Foundational Values

As I reflect on the foundational values upon which we have built our lives and our business, I remember growing up in a greatly diverse neighborhood consisting of many socio-economic classes. Doctors, lawyers, and teachers lived right next to janitors, laborers, and even those on welfare. Of course, their houses were different and the professionals had large and stately homes while others had much more humble forms of shelter. So as a child I observed what was possible as well as the plight of being at various levels of poverty.

I saw my own parents change our house from almost a shack without central heat or air conditioning into a home with central heat, and city water instead of well water. We never had central air conditioning. For many years my Dad would arrive home after work and work on the house. He installed central heat by removing the pot belly stove, raising the floor, and installing piping for the registers that would provide central heat to the whole house. He installed the furnace and eventually changed the pipes providing water so that he could remove the pump providing well water and set the stage for city water.

It was a tremendous amount of work, but over the years my parents continued to make improvements on the house as time, Dad's expertise, and money allowed. It was never like a fully constructed house done by a builder, and was never completed but I was never uncomfortable even when there was no central heat. We managed and continued to grow as a family.

One of the key values was that my grandmother and parents would often discuss and comment on the importance of education to achieve a "better life." Grandmother, who married and had her first child at thirteen, taught herself to read. My father dropped out of school at twelve to begin work to assist his parents because he had thirteen siblings. Because of my maternal grandmother's belief in education, she ensured all of her children received a high school diploma. They never had a vision of college for themselves because they were so poor that work for survival was more important, but they definitely had that vision for their children.

They were not envious or resentful of those financially better, but sought ways to improve themselves through hard work and family support. As a result, there was nothing more important than school. I was taught through their actions and words that work and school were not negotiable and had to be valued. The only reason to miss either was if one were in the hospital or dead. No excuses like a headache or stomachache were appropriate for anyone that wanted to improve their life. Hard work and education were key along with continuous learning and using the knowledge acquired.

Their solution was to look within themselves to improve, not towards how we could blame others for what we did not have. They understood their situation, but did not accept being "stuck" in their present state. They continued to improve their life and demonstrated these values: Do not be a victim and be accountable for our own decisions. It was important to observe "the world" and determine what actions (moral, legal, and ethical) were required to reach our goals.

As a result of this foundation, I began to observe and listen to any and everyone that I admired, looking for clues, ideas, and methods to lead a life of continuous improvement. It was very early in my life that it became evident that nothing was more important than education to have any "professional" career. So the first short term goal became getting through high school without getting pregnant. I observed that pregnancy in high school or when unwed was a gigantic "show stopper" and a huge impediment in improving life and getting better jobs as an adult.

In the book, "Kids Having Kids, Economic Costs and Social Consequences of Teen Pregnancy," edited by, Rebecca A. Maynard, it documents that poverty rates were much higher in teen mothers. 80 percent of teen mothers received welfare during ten years following the birth of their first child, 44 percent of them for more than five years. However, I did not need a study or research to realize those facts because I could simply look around my neighborhood and school to see the life impacts of teen pregnancy. Some girls from more affluent families were able to avoid extreme poverty by living with or being subsidized by their parents, but the impact on life was still very present and very observable.

College was also an obvious requirement for attaining a "professional" career. Of course, there was trade school or other ways to achieve added education to provide a better path to solid and well-paying jobs, but my parents often talked about the "white collar" jobs with admiration. Therefore, my aspirations were to achieve what I knew would make them proud and would lead to my own life goals.

I was also taught that "where there is a will there is a way" through the ups and downs experienced by my parents as they changed direction when things were not going as planned or expected. They showed me that if God plants the seed then He will provide the means for growth. Additionally, while work may be required, *God's way and path are not confusing and will not require a violation of His laws nor the laws of man.*[7]

Choosing Your Peers

I was also taught to be very careful about who I have as friends or close

> **As Jim Rohn said, "You become the average of the five people you spend the most time with."**

[7] See Hebrews 13:17

acquaintances. If they are just like me, would I learn anything new? If they are struggling with relationships, weight, finances or positive behaviors, they might cause me to lose focus and negatively influence me. If they are doing what I perceive as better or where I want to be, I can learn and improve.

Whether it is health, income, relationships and/or happiness, the people you hang out with are strongly reflected in your life. If you improve the quality of your peer group it will have a direct effect on every other area of your life. Learn from them by choosing peers that are reflective of "good," and choose those pursuing excellence in one or various areas of life that is important to you. Humbly keep in mind that no human is perfect, but attempt to move towards elements that are aligned and seeking to be more like the Lord. You could almost read the following scripture but instead of the words "whatever is" you could replace them with "whoever is," excellent or praiseworthy, learn these things from them.

Finally, brothers and sisters, whatever is true, whatever is noble, whatever is right, whatever is pure, whatever is lovely, whatever is admirable—if anything is excellent or praiseworthy—think about such things. (Philippians 4:8)

Nuggets for Living Fully and Successfully

Never let others define you.

When one knows the Lord, they want to follow Christian principals and neither pride nor arrogance is part of those principals.

Define yourself using the Christian principals you believe are the most important to build your life upon. Rationale: Christian principals have proven sound for centuries. When science is repeatable and substantiated over mire decades it is deemed true. Therefore, I contend that since Christian principals have withstood the tests of time for centuries, their effectiveness for living a fruitful life is valid.

As Jim Rohn said, "You become the average of the five people you spend the most time with."

Who are the five people (outside of family) with whom you spend the most time?

What are they helping you to "become"?

What are they helping you to accomplish?

Are they pursuing excellence in an important area impacting your life?

Is it the person you really want to "become"?

Are you allowing others to define you?

Life Together in Air Force Has Scott Couple Flying High (Metro-East Journal September 14, 1978 by Jean Ann Bailey

"Religion also plays a major role in their lives. Although they are non-denominational—Brenda was bought up Baptist and Maurice, Methodist—Brenda feels the main thing is to find a place in which anyone can serve the Lord as they see best."

Chapter 9

PATHS DIRECTED

The Simple Path
Silence is Prayer
Prayer is Faith
Faith is Love
Love is Service
The Fruit of Service is Peace
– Mother Teresa

As I reflect back, I realize that the Lord has always been intimately involved in my life. Some people call it luck while others use words like fate or chance, and still others may actually think it is the result of being super special and smart. However, I could not have positioned myself for the many positive or challenging things in life so I know the Lord has been directing my path.

I believe the Lord is very personal for everyone; so we are only able to speak from own personal experience with God. I have experienced substantial material, emotional, and spiritual blessings, and I have also had my share of what I consider challenges. My challenges may seem lame or trivial to some and difficult to others. Our challenges are based on our relationship with the Lord, and His determination of what we need or can bear with the purpose of glorifying and bringing us closer to Him. Permit me to further explain what I mean.

I pray and speak to the Lord often. Certainly I do not believe that God is a "Santa Claus," but I also do not believe He is the cause of our suffering. Some of it is based on decisions we have made. Good biblical decisions tend to lead to great life consequences while decisions that destroy the body, mind or spirit of one's self or others such as drugs, promiscuous sex, cheating, killing, lying, etc. tend to lead to horrible life consequences.

Some difficulties cause "godly" people to look at the downtrodden and reach out in brotherly love. Other difficulties position one to better counsel or relate to others. We often find the best counselors for drug or alcohol addicted people are former drug or alcohol addicted people. Humans often believe unless one has been in their "shoes" they cannot possibly understand what they are going through.

Anyway, even though I am only three years from my last cancer treatment, the side effects still cause concern. That is my cross to bear. Am I angry with God? No. Do I question "why me?" Yes, I am

Bottom line, I strongly believe that God has a reason, season, and purpose for everything.

sorry to say that I do though I should not. The reason I should not ask the "why me" question is because when things were good from a human prospective I did not question "why me." Well, sometimes I actually did in sincere gratefulness. I really do thank God for His blessings and wonder why I am so blessed. Then I reflect and know that any blessings I have received were to glorify the Lord and not for my own comfort. Often my

---

[8] See Ecclesiastes 3:1-8

challenges are simply not about me either. Depending on how challenges are handled and overcome, they also can glorify God.

When certain achievements were reached or when I was recognized publicly, that experience often gave others faith or hope. Emails or other communications often come from people from my past expressing what a difference I made in their life. I have always tried to let them know that God was the reason for whatever positive inspiration they were obtaining.

Once when I presented at a business presentation, I expressed how I wake up each morning at 4:30 or 5:00 a.m. and read scripture, pray, work out, fix breakfast, and then shower to prepare for work. A business owner came up to me afterwards and asked if I really did that. She was shocked and somewhat unbelieving that I included God at the very start of my day. She walked away questioning if that really was the "secret to my business success," but indicated that she would like to have faith enough to do those same things. Several months later, she sent me an email just to let me know that she had begun having lunch with an associate to read scripture and pray. She noted that her life was more peaceful and her business doing better as a result. That is an example of God working through me to touch others for His glory.

The Lord is my personal savior, my guide, my protector, and my prince of peace, and He has been with me through my blessings and challenges. Please understand that I also believe for God to work in our lives, we must diligently read His word, seek His direction, and try to stay away from the negative human earthly traps.

If we seek Him first He will guide and direct our paths.

---

[9] See Proverbs 3:6

Obviously God Directed

It was fall and the start of the school year. I was only fourteen years old. I saw Maurice down the long hall in high school. He was not the most handsome young man, not a jock, not affluent, and not an intelligent nerd, but my heart flipped when I saw him. He wore a short sleeved sweat shirt and slacks. He had glasses and a short haircut. He did not even notice me. I would watch him perched at the end of the hall and I swooned inside. Even now forty-seven years later I remember and still have the same feelings in my heart and body. Since it has been such a long and wonderful journey, I can now say he is my soulmate.

As part of my school activities, I was selling programs to the football game and saw it as a chance to speak to him.

I went up to him and asked, "Would you like to buy a program?"

His response was, "I already know who is playing."

I would learn later that he actually did not have any money because he had to save it for lunches. Finally, after letting some friends know that I "liked" him, he called me. I was thrilled. We talked for months, but I knew he was calling other girls as well. I remember praying that if God felt this was the one for me, then to please bring him to me in the right way. I backed off and watched from afar.

When I was almost sixteen, he started calling me again. When that occurred, I realized that the Lord had graced me with an answer to my prayer. Naturally, I was not sure of our total future, but I trusted God and vowed **We all must make prayerful decisions and accept the consequences trusting God.** to trust and remain faithful because God had heard my prayer. To this day, I have kept that vow to God and when we married, I kept that vow to Maurice.

I respect Maurice as head of the family. He is a strong believer and I have always felt he would treat me and our family Christ-like to the best of his ability. Therefore, I follow his direction believing it comes from his relationship with the Lord.

However, I do not just follow blindly. We discuss at length decisions that will cause a change in direction or location. Maurice as the head of our home was and is the ultimate decision maker, and I do not care what society says about the roles of men and women. He is much stronger than I am in so very many ways. He has also respected me and my gifts so we actually complement each other just as God intended. I am more globally oriented while he is more detailed oriented. In a room of many people, I can pick up on several conversations at once while he is more likely to pay close attention to the key reason we are at the event.

When Maurice came home talking about joining the Air Force, it just felt right. It would provide a means to complete our education, so how could I put anything in place to block it? Others thought we were nuts! There were so many horror stories about the outcomes and impact on lives of those who served in the Vietnam era. In hindsight, joining the Air Force together was definitely God inspired and was very important for our lives together. The Vietnam War was not yet over, but just a couple of months after we joined it was. God took care of that.

When we could not go to Officer's Training School because I was expecting our first child, Maurice did not get upset. He suggested we accept the honorable discharge at the end of our six year enlistment because "we would be alright." I was frightened because in the Air Force we were guaranteed food and shelter. Not so in civilian life. There were no guarantees and we were about to have our first child, but I trusted Maurice and God.

Before we received our final Air Force pay checks, Maurice had found a civilian job. It was exciting yet frightening. We also found it was a great deal more expensive to live as a civilian, but we had faith that all would be well.

As we looked for apartments in St. Louis, we were not exactly welcomed. Openings disappeared once we arrived and they saw that we were Black. We did not get discouraged or angry and found a place further out from Maurice's work than we had hoped, but it was fine. When they announced a short year later that we had to buy the unit we were renting or move, we chose to move. Maurice and I discussed expanding our horizons to search for a house. We peacefully lived and raised our children in that home for over thirty years. Maurice kept the property in excellent condition, and we remodeled it a couple of times. Little did I realize what was next as God directed Maurice along our path.

Maurice suggested moving to Clayton, Missouri. In God's timing, we were led to a wonderful condo in Clayton that was to be our downsizing since the children were grown and out of the house. Once we were settled in Clayton, Maurice began to think about moving to a warmer climate. In our early pre-children days, we had actually discussed and requested to be stationed in Florida among other warm climates. It really sounded great to have a getaway in a warmer climate since we were now older. Due to the 2008 economic crisis, much of the real estate in 2011 was extremely underpriced.

Maurice searched for foreclosures and asked a neighbor about a Florida community. As God does things, not only had they heard about it, that was exactly where they had bought and spent their winters. That neighbor invited us to visit and stay with them while we looked at properties. We accepted the invitation and looked at over thirty properties during that

long weekend. We found the perfect condo for us and proceeded to purchase it. We then awaited the process to move towards closing.

An Alarming Challenge

In the meantime, we attended a holiday party at the St. Louis condo
where we found that one of the people that lived in the building was a
dermatologist. Since the dentists involved had diagnosed my tongue as
oral lichen planus, which I read could be related to the dermis and meno-
pause in women, we asked her if she could take a look. She suggested that
I make an appointment.

Christmas was coming and we were to travel to participate in a marathon with our youngest daughter in Hawaii that January. She ran a full
marathon while Maurice and I ran a half marathon. Upon returning to
St. Louis, I called for an appointment with our dermatologist neighbor.

She took one look, said it was not oral lichen planus, and strongly
urged me to go to a specialist she recommended. I sent her an email to
thank her and to let her know that the recommended doctor would not
be available for two months. She responded immediately saying that I
should not wait that long and had called another specialist to get me an
appointment. I was not aware how serious a situation it was, but she was
concerned enough to quickly act on my behalf. I believe God led us to
move to Clayton to meet that neighbor who saved my life.

I went to her recommended Otolaryngologist who specialized in surgery including head and neck cancers. We closed on the Florida property
on February 1st. My first appointment with the specialist was the very
next day. The doctor took one look and diagnosed it as squamous cell
carcinoma. He had not staged it yet, but knew from experience it was

important to quickly address the cancer. He asked if I would be available for surgery on the very next Wednesday. Little did we know it was Stage IV.

After the surgery and treatments, Maurice booked our flight to Florida so I could get away and rest as well as heal. It was hard for me to rest when in St. Louis because besides serving on two public boards, I served on many non-profit boards, was the chair of a university board of trustees, and involved with various informal mentorships. While I was in the hospital and going through the chemo and radiation treatments, Maurice proceeded to use the Internet to ensure the Florida condo was set up and ready for us. My last radiation treatment was April 23 and by mid-May, we were on a flight from St. Louis to Florida where the humidity served to keep my dry mouth moisturized since my salivary glands were impacted greatly by the radiation. As it turn out, the condo was a godsend which allowed me to rest and reflect on our life journey as I healed. It also allowed time to begin the process of writing this book.

Had we stayed in our St. Peter's home we would not have met that dermatologist neighbor. Thankfully God, through Maurice ensured that we moved to Clayton and we received the critical referral. Though I did not understand it at the time and thought it frivolous to own a Florida condo, had we not closed on the condo in Florida when we did, I would not have found my place of healing.

Are you ready for more? Just one and a half years later at Christmas at her home, our eldest daughter inquired why we traveled back and forth when we seemed to enjoy Florida better and found it improved our health. I really liked our St. Louis condo and disregarded her comment. However, God was setting us up to be open minded to what He had planned for the next phase of our life journey.

Just three weeks later, Maurice got a call from the St. Louis condo developer asking if an associate and possible buyer could see the condo.

 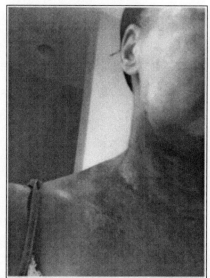

Chemo and Radiation

We said we were not interested in selling, but they could look. Well, they liked it and wanted to buy it. They made an offer a couple of times and finally Maurice and I agreed to sell realizing God was directing us because it was not something we were seeking. It was a win all around for the buyer and for us. As a result, we began living in Florida year round where we could finally become consistent in going to just one church instead of attending services in each place. We could also become more involved in the community. Prior to that it was like having a foot in each place without a commitment to either church "home."

In All Thy Ways Acknowledge Him and He Shall Direct Thy Path

People are often surprised when they find out we did not have a goal to be where we are materially speaking. Although we are "well off," we never sought, believed or dreamed to be in such a situation. We just worked hard and tried our best to "do the right things" as we followed the path before us.

We were both brought up in a lower middle-class environment and were blessed with a two-parent household. My family and Maurice's family refused to take welfare because they were blessed with health and our mothers had a high school education. They were proud people, in a good way, doing the hard work necessary to make a living and support the family. Our basic needs came from employment and hard work which even allowed for a few special things like a car, a treat of ice cream once in a while, dance lessons, recreation like bowling or roller skating, and a few new clothes at the start of a school year.

Point being, we were just two generations from slavery and share-croppers so we had no goal or dream to have these material blessings! We did not express to each other or anyone a goal of building a multi-million dollar business, owing properties or driving luxury cars. Those were not goals or aspirations. Our hard work was for food, shelter, clothing, a solid education for our daughters, and to stay healthy and financially sound so we would not be a burden to our children in old age. We wanted to work and never be fired. We wanted to be independent and not be a burden to society. The success was simply the result.

What occurred was that as we moved along the path, God provided the foundational necessities along the way to include knowledge, mentors, guidance, and a view of possibilities that seemed impossible from such "normal" and humble beginnings. We did not look at the material acquisitions or blessings of others with anger or resentment, but sought to understand the "how" so that if their way was moral, ethical, and legal we could learn from them.

The Path

First, it was the promise to our hard working parents to complete our education. That was critical for a life that was not impoverished.

Taking care of everything with which we were blessed meant the blessings continued to flow. Like our parents, we kept our cars clean and spotless, our clothes clean and tasteful, and our homes clean and tidy. This was not because we worshiped them, but because we believed everything we received was a gift from God. Therefore, it was important to properly take care of those gifts.

Working hard work for our employers using the good work ethics our parents instilled in us not only provided income, but job security and promotion.

Taking total responsibility for our children ensuring they had a stable home life, we never lost sight of our responsibilities and goals nor our love for one another.

Taking care of ourselves physically was a high priority. People often teased or chided me for working so hard or exercising so much, but I was grateful to have the energy and ability. I never wanted to waste it so I took advantage of every opportunity even when it stretched me far beyond what I thought possible.

As we reached certain milestones, we would add materially. Buying a home and committing to paying off the mortgage early was a huge milestone. We did not know exactly how to accomplish this, but we knew debt was not good biblically nor was it comfortable so we patiently worked and paid the monthly mortgage. Not knowing how to accomplish that goal did not stop us from making improvements and doing the necessary upkeep to the house such as replacing the roof after twenty-five years, replacing worn appliances, and adding a fence among other things as money and time allowed. Since we did not walk in the house with shoes on, our flooring lasted for twenty-seven years, and even then we only replaced the carpeting in the early 2000s because it was sculptured shag from the seventies and extremely retro in a negative way according to our daughters.

Taking care of the material blessings "allowed" for more blessings because we were able to sell most things for a small profit or lovingly give them away even after using them for many years because they were "gently worn." We truly believed that our blessings were to bless others once we took care of our own major responsibilities entrusted to us.

The result of staying focused on the major "right" things actually led to more blessings! While in the Air Force, we did not know if we would be remaining in the service after our six year enlistment, but we knew that would be a decision point. Newly married with steady pay checks and jobs was great, but rather than spending all that we made, we saved my entire pay. Once in a while we would splurge for a trip to Costa del Sol or the Canary Islands, after all we were in Spain, young and vibrant! We did not want to waste the opportunity to experience the culture, but saving was important to us.

We knew next to a home, a car was a major expense. After learning of a program to send new cars from Europe to the U.S. at greatly reduced costs we planned for and then paid cash for a new Volvo! At the time, it was one of the safest and most reliable cars so that is what we thought we wanted and needed. It did not use all of our savings either. We also bought some very good solid furniture that was not trendy but classic. It lasted twenty-seven or so years! In hindsight, that was a good decision since we knew we would have to rent housing upon returning to the U.S. We did not know where we would be stationed upon return. We were able to eliminate some major expenses by being frugal and focused on the items that would result in the best lasting value.

Of course, if we had never joined the Air Force and conscientiously saved our money, none of this would have been possible. Since we knew we had to complete our education, we continued to take classes towards that goal while in Spain. While we enjoyed ourselves immensely, we did not allow the fun and clubs in Madrid to derail our focus. We took time for fun, but worked diligently to complete our undergraduate degrees while in Spain, and then we both attained our Master's Degrees upon our return to the United States.

When buying a home, an older co-worker who owned a home that we admired suggested we buy the most home we could afford just in case we had to live there for thirty years. Little did we know that advice teamed with the goal and reality of paying off the mortgage in less than sixteen years would be so important as we continued down our life path together.

Also important was staying married and committed to our overall goals. These decisions led to starting the business and continuing to live according to God's direction.

As our lives changed and savings as well as circumstances allowed, after tithing and giving to charity we would invest in material things for ourselves, things we never dreamed possible.

As you navigate, making right decisions is critical. So how does one do that?

Nuggets for Living Fully and Successfully

The lesson here is to have small goals that might lead to your dreams and concentrate on achieving those intermediate goals to move towards the larger goals.

What are some of your small goals? Where do they lead?

Do not dwell on how or what to do, but follow the lessons, mentors, and paths the Lord places before you.

What lessons and mentors have the Lord placed in your path?
How have these positioned you for your future? Your spiritual future?
Your family future? Your educational future? Your career future?

Remember to acknowledge His mercy, grace, and blessings (Proverbs 3:6).

Do you acknowledge and thank God for His mercy and grace in times of blessings and in times of challenges?

Are you faithfully caring for the blessings God has already given you?
In taking care for your material blessings, ensure you do not allow those material blessings to become literal or figurative idols in your life.

Humbly, faithfully, and decidedly navigate the landscape. Look for God's compass directing your paths.

Describe how you are doing this in your own life.

Taking the High Road-*CEO Brenda Newberry stays focused on integrity as she builds a successful business* (*St. Louis Woman Magazine,* March 2007 by Susan Fadem)

"My mother is all about perseverance and faith in God," says Yasmin Newberry Cline. "My mom is a role model: working out, eating healthy, going to church, and focusing on education," adds Cherie Newberry, now completing her master's degree in education as well as teaching school.

Chapter 10

DECISION MAKING

So it is, when a person views life through the "lens of truth," they are better able to discern the "hidden" truth and distinguish what is right from wrong. -Josh McDowell, *Right from Wrong*

S ince I was majority owner of the company as recommended by the attorney at the company start-up, I was the ultimate decision maker. It did not present a problem as we grew the company. Most of the time, Maurice and I came to consensus. I respected Maurice greatly. We always communicated and came to solutions and resolutions for the various challenges that surfaced. There were many. After all it was a small business and we had to work with and for people, not machines.

There was one particular time in which we absolutely did not agree. Our company had become a subcontractor to a larger business that had "graduated" from the 8(a) Minority Program and had grown substantially over the years. They were able to utilize the fact that we were a minority and female-owned small business to fulfill their requirement for diversity inclusion on government contracts. Through the small business office, they officially became our mentor and we were their protégé. There were many benefits available through this arrangement such as assistance in the purchase and installation of advanced financial systems and various certifications to position our company to compete more successfully. Unfortunately, they often treated us as competitors rather than partners or even protégées. There were many ups and downs in the relationship and sometimes it seemed as if they considered us a threat, but more often than not, it was cordial with underpinnings of contention.

Maurice warned me to cease doing business with them and to phase out of the relationship. We had often discussed their questionable treatment. There was a very poignant morning when we were walking after having completed a five mile run.

Maurice said, "You just do not understand why I say not to work with them."

My response was, "I understand you. I just do not agree."

Maurice then gave up and honored our positioning with respect to company ownership, "Do what you think is best."

I proceeded to do business with this vendor mostly because of the strong relationship our business developer had with them. There was a contract coming up for rebid. They had been awarded this contract for the past nine years. The government agency decided to re-bid it under a General Services Administration Schedule. This meant that only companies with a GSA schedule could bid. Since we had a GSA schedule we were eligible to bid on our own, but realized teaming with a larger company was better positioning.

Well, this prime vendor wanted us to team up with them as a subcontractor on the contract. They knew the work intimately due to their long term experience. Given that, everyone considered they were a sure fire favorite. Under the then current contract, they subcontracted about five of the contract positions with us out of the sixty positions on the contract.

The agency knew of us and our work due to the other GSA contract we had been awarded a couple of years prior. The proposal they were submitting offered us two positions for the life of the contract. We understood that the contract being bid was for only about thirty positions initially, but was subject to great growth. Therefore, we suggested and requested 10 percent instead of only two positions for the life of the contract. They refused. After many discussions back and forth, they refused to budge from two positions. Two days before the proposal was due, they finally gave us an ultimatum saying you get two positions, take it or leave it. To everyone's surprise, I said leave it. They submitted their bid without including us.

Months before, something in my heart told me to prepare our own proposal for this contract. I did not let anyone on staff know because I was hoping the prime vendor would change their position in their relationship with us. They did not. So I put the finishing touches on our proposal and submitted it. Maurice was aware, but thought I was foolish. He felt it was a large contract and there was no way they would award us the contract.

Lo and behold, the agency awarded us the contract! Everyone was astonished and of course our team was surprised as well as thrilled, at least until the prime vendor refused to cooperate. As common practice with government contracts with high security level requirements, they were to release their staff on the contract to the winning vendor which was us. They refused. They threatened their staff with lawsuits if any of them worked for us. They made the next few months a "living hell!" Over time, things settled down and they finally released the applicable staff and our team managed the contract. Ultimately, Maurice was correct. We should have discontinued the relationship earlier on.

Skin in the Game in Several Ways

Just as Maurice and I both had financial interests in the company and considered carefully each decision, we knew it was important that our children have a stake in decisions as well. "Skin in the game" so to speak.

When both girls were young, we often told them college was not an option unless they did well enough in school to get scholarships to attend.

> **Being committed means having something to gain and something to lose based on the outcome of a decision.**

Our oldest was a junior in high school when I resigned from MasterCard. Because I was not working outside the home with a boss and a schedule, I was able drive our oldest daughter to various interviews for college entry and scholarships. The result was that due to her hard work in school, she was accepted everywhere she applied and offered scholarships to her preferred choices. One offer was for a full academic scholarship and that was the one she accepted.

She made excellent grades and graduated cum laude with a bachelor's degree in broadcast journalism. Before graduation, she decided that she wanted to attend law school. Maurice and I were supportive, but also shocked because she had rebutted every attempt we had made to suggest that she go to law school. The deal made was that she could go, but she had to obtain the loans. She followed through. What was interesting was that when she was in her second year of law school, she asked to meet with us and announced that law school was too hard and she wanted to quit. Maurice and I exchanged glances and told her we supported her decision, but the loans remained hers. She would need employment to pay them off. Needless to say a few days later she told us she was going to continue. She not only graduated from law school, but also passed the bar the first time. Our graduation gift was to provide her the funds to pay off the loans.

We had two girls and that meant when they were ready, we would have two weddings for which to pay—hopefully not at the same time. A friend of ours gave us an excellent suggestion. He said either promise the same dollar amounts to each child for

Had she not had "skin in the game," she may not have made the decision to persevere when the going got tough.

their weddings or just tell them we would match the dollars they were willing to "bring to the table." Since the value of money changes over the years due to the economy, promising a certain amount of money could lead to debates over the value of money at the time. Therefore, we told both girls that we would match the financial resources they wanted to spend on their wedding.

The logic of this is that neither child would be able to say we loved one over the other due to the cost, size or other variables of their weddings. Our expenditure was solely based on the financial resources they had earned and set aside. Naturally the longer they waited to wed, the greater the possibilities they would have more financial resources. It was also conceivable that if they were older with a career then their fiancée would also have a career and be in the position to contribute in some way to their wedding beyond the basic groom responsibilities.

When our oldest was picking out her wedding dress at the bridal shop, I overheard a woman in her late thirties that had been married over ten years complaining because her parents gave her sister a much larger wedding. She expressed her jealously because she felt they loved her sister more just based on the size of their weddings. It was amazing to me that so many years later that woman was still upset. I realized the wisdom of our agreement of matching the funds our daughters wanted to commit to their weddings.

Our agreement with our girls was definitely a nice way of ensuring that our daughters would not base their opinion of our love simply on what we spent for their weddings. It was based solely on their decisions and timing. We did not feel our ego or self-esteem or success was based on how large a wedding we could showcase to our friends and associates.

As it turned out, it was a good process. Our oldest daughter was married in the summer between her second and third year of law school. Her fiancée was working

> **The life lesson of decision making amidst financial constraints was more important for our daughters to learn than trying to impress others with a showcase wedding.**

on his Ph.D. in mechanical engineering. Needless to say their funds were limited. She did, however, obtain a great summer internship at a law firm and was able to save for the wedding. As promised, we matched or paid half of all expenses. Our wedding gift, however, was to reimburse her in full the dollars she spent on the wedding. It was a great surprise for her, but the process served to ensure she carefully considered each and every expense for her beautiful day. It was not the most lavish wedding nor was it like that of a pauper, but it was a very intimate and beautiful wedding.

By contrast, our youngest daughter had a much different wedding. Once she had graduated with her degree in business finance, she then decided she wanted to serve in the "Teach for America" program rather than going straight into a graduate degree program. Interestingly enough, I had just had a presentation from some very impressive young people who had completed their service with "Teach for America." As a result, God had prepared me to be supportive when she called letting me know of her desire to serve. Otherwise my reaction might have been to provide her the choice of getting a "real" job or going to graduate school.

She did her two years of service with "Teach for America" which was extremely challenging. In fact, in the beginning, she called us several times literally in tears because it was so difficult teaching over twenty inner city children in a classroom solo. When I offered her the suggestion to quit, her response was, "No, we Newberry's do not quit."

As it turned out, during the program they offered her the opportunity to complete her graduate degree in teaching. To shed some light on this decision, when she was beginning her freshman year of college, she expressed a desire to major in psychology because she wanted to work with and help children. Maurice and I we were okay with that major provided she would promise to get her doctorate degree. From what we understood, the field of psychology had very little promise of good job prospects without an advanced degree. Well, about her second week of her freshman year, she called home to share with us that she really enjoyed college, but did not see herself staying there for the nine or ten years it would take to complete a Ph.D. She was changing her major to business finance. Of course, we gladly supported that decision.

So the process of service with "Teach for America" teamed with a Master's degree in Early Childhood Education really moved her towards the goal of helping children. Of course, the mission of "Teach for America" was to interest those that may not have majored in teaching to fall in love with it during their service and stay in education. In our daughter's case it was mission accomplished!

Following the two years of service and the acquisition of the graduate degree in Early Childhood Education, she determined that she enjoyed education but wanted to have more global impact by concentrating on the administration aspects. After working for the YWCA part-time during challenging economic times, she was hired to be the assistant center coordinator of a Head Start center. A couple of years later she became the

Center Coordinator of a smaller Head Start location. So, this was the start of her career.

This process meant that she was older and had employment for several years before she was engaged. Therefore, she had greater savings with which to use for her wedding. It was also a beautiful wedding. It was what is referred to as a destination wedding on a beach. The wedding was still a small intimate wedding, but with a beach location—more expensive, but with only about twenty people attending. She later paid half for a reception in our hometown. In keeping with our tradition, our wedding gift to her was to reimburse her for her half of the wedding and reception expenses.

I have been sharing insights following the path set before you and making right commitments along the way. Other discoveries in navigating life's landscape are important. I want now to share some of those with you.

Both daughters received the lesson and accepted their responsibility for planning and paying their half of the wedding they planned along the way.

Nuggets for Living Fully and Successfully

Being committed means having something to gain and something to lose based on the outcome of a decision.

How has this helped change the way you are going to make important decisions in the future whether business or personal?

Had our daughter not had "skin in the game," she may not have made the decision to persevere.

Describe how having "skin in the game" is going to help you in your future decision making.

How would you explain this important concept to help others, especially your own children?

The life lesson of decision making amidst financial constraints was more important.

What life lesson did you learn from this chapter in the area of decision making?

When we invest significantly, i.e. buy in, we are much more likely to stay in and be "all in."

What have you learned about commitment in yourself and others when one's investment in a venture, relationship, or project is low?

Life priorities empower us to succeed and finish strong like getting an education, staying fit, eating healthy, loving others, growing spiritually, and becoming a learner for life.

What are your life priorities and how are they working or not working for you?

Taking the High Road: *CEO Brenda Newberry stays focused on integrity as she builds a successful business* (St. Louis Woman Magazine March 2007 by Susan Fadem)

"Once you compromise your integrity, you can never get it back!"
– Brenda Newberry

Chapter 11

NAVIGATING THE LANDSCAPE

Smooth seas do not make skillful sailors.   — African Proverb

While a teen, my mother pointed out how white girls that were sexually promiscuous would not be considered loose or whores but "colored girls" were. I was told of stories from slave times where the slave girl was blamed if the master violated her. The straight and narrow was the preferred way for me to behave. I had the sacrifices of generations to represent. Actually, we all do. Everyone represents the generations of family members and regardless of the plight, successes or crimes of those of the past, we can make a difference and choose to represent them reverently.

Additionally, the Air Force added to those values, work ethic and attitudes. Our joint "mission" was to do well and "do no harm." Once we had children, our mission was to bring up healthy, well adjusted, independent adults that were equipped to add value to the world. We wanted to follow Christian principals because they worked. When the girls became older and it seemed as if there simply were never enough hours in the day or week, we did not go to church on Sundays, but our commitment towards the mission and our faith remained strong. Those early lessons never left and later we did resume our faithful church attendance.

Some of the things we sought to accomplish were to create a life so that we would not be a burden to our children in our old age, to be debt free early in life, to honor each other and our marriage vows, and do all as if for the Lord. This was a tall order. We did not know that those were some key goals that actually led to successful and peaceful lives. We just trusted and knew that with God all things are possible. We still strongly hold that belief. We did not have to know exactly the "how" because God would provide the paths along the way. We only needed to honor and glorify the Lord and He would help us navigated through whatever the landscape.

Later in life, I was exposed to the writings of Robert Kiyosaki, "Rich Dad Poor Dad" and "Cash Flow Game." Some of the concepts of the game were biblical, but a casual observer would not recognize that fact. Concepts such as if you tithe or give to charity you get an extra turn, if you divorce you lose all your money and start over, if you "invest" in what he termed "do-dads" you get behind, if you invest in appreciating assets you gain and achieve more net worth, and if you have children you increase your monthly expenditures. The ultimate message is to establish as a goal to live a life of good decisions so one "gets out of the rat race," greatly reduces or eliminates debt, and becomes able to live on investments rather than from paycheck to paycheck.

The other critical lesson was that it did not matter what your job was at the beginning of the game. If you followed solid life principles, then a janitor could actually get out of the "rat race" more rapidly than a doctor, attorney or pilot. It taught good decision making. We all know that stress is associated with living beyond one's means, dealing with blended families, and doing things that destroy your body or family. Life is hard and challenging enough without added stress, and any lessons that demonstrate ways to reduce or prevent it are definitely helpful.

Biblical Principles Work in Life and Business

I have discovered that if we would actually try to follow the lessons in the Bible, we would have a peaceful life that contributes to society. If we would really love our neighbor as ourselves and think of everyone as our neighbor, we would not lie, cheat, steal, kill, covet their material things, commit adultery, have idols, and would rest at least one day of the week. Rest was a lesson that took me far too many years to learn, but that principle is extremely important.

Just think what it would be like if no one was angry with you and you could live life without being stressed! Some people have a view that being Christian is a life of being guilt ridden, but I strongly believe it actually creates freedom. Imagine if you never have to compare and desire the material things of others. Imagine if you do not need to worry about getting a sexually transmitted disease. Think of the freedom of not having any envy or jealously because a mentor is more than happy to share the way they achieved success. Imagine never having to worry about the stacking of your lies or the things you have said about others coming back to haunt you. Imagine having a trust so strong with your spouse that you never have to worry about infidelity. Imagine never stealing and creating a criminal record. Imagine never killing and not having to worry about retaliation by individuals or entire countries. Imagine yourself in a lifestyle of being grateful and accepting the material gifts from the Lord after tithing and receiving His promise of blessings too numerous to store.

Understanding these things early in life due to parents, church, education, and the Air Force positioned us to move towards our goals with peace and love for others. They made our goals easy to establish though not always easy to accomplish. After all, we were and remain human and not even close to perfect. God knows we made mistakes!

While in the Air Force, we made a point of working and doing our best. As we became accustomed to civilian life, we continued and tried to work as if for God and not for our bosses or those around us. We tried to ignore and not participate in gossip. We learned as much as possible and remained vigilant so that we were aware of opportunities. We tried to support and respect our bosses as much as possible.

These are just a few examples of the peace and freedom we can experience in life if we choose to live according to the biblical principles presented to us in the Bible.

We were brought up and continue to respect law enforcement. We knew that some in law enforcement were not favorable towards African Americans, but also knew they were the exception not the rule. Unfortunately, we grew up observing fire hoses and the like turned on "colored people" during the late '50s into the '60s, so our respect for the law was teamed with a good dose of fear of repercussion. Therefore, we were not inclined to put ourselves in a position that would cause us to be confronted by law enforcement.

Our babysitters were mostly young girls so when they needed to be driven home after babysitting for us, I would drive them home. No need for Maurice to be stopped by police because he was a black man in a white neighborhood with a young girl in is car. We were prudent in all that we did so as not to even give the appearance of impropriety.

Maurice coached our daughter's high school track teams. He took the time to get certified. When the oldest graduated, he stopped until our youngest began running track and then coached again until she graduated. Those days there were several incidences of young girls falsely accusing their male coaches or teachers of sexual advances and there were also cases of actual inappropriate behavior. Therefore, Maurice saw no need to place himself in any situation where he might be compromised. When he coached, our daughters were visibly present.

When Maurice had to drive at night through a predominately white neighborhood to pick up our oldest daughter, I would awaken our youngest so we could accompany him. This lessened the chance of him being stopped by the police. When he was stopped for "routine checks" while doing nothing wrong, Maurice was very careful to be respectful. Some might call this "selling out," but it was simply navigating the landscape to avoid trouble.

Even in our sixties, we are aware of the landscape. We were out to dinner with two other couples that happened to be white. One of them volunteered to take care of the tip. Maurice immediately paused thinking that was not such a good idea. He felt it would be perpetuating the stereotype that blacks do not tip because a tip would not be with our payment. So we had the waiter open the checks to see that none of us put the tip on the check. The waiter laughed when he saw that the last check contained the tip for all of us. The point was made. Something so simple it was laughable and yet shameful that the stereotype still exists and is verbally discussed in many circles. *Overkill?* Perhaps, but this is an example of navigating the landscape. No need for that waiter to think blacks don't tip.

> "It has never been enough for me to just be good at what I did. I was determined to give my best and go the extra mile. I strove for excellence." – Brenda Newberry

During our work life, it was important that we surveyed the boss often to ensure we were meeting or exceeding expectations. This way no one is surprised at review time and at the same time it showed we cared enough to ensure our performance was solid. These are just a few examples of being aware of the landscape and positioning our lives to navigate towards and into safe waters.

No Victim Mentality

We continued to observe positive people, role models or those who had accomplished what we admired. Asking or looking for how others reached what we admired helped us to set our personal goals. We never considered being angry or jealous nor did we think they owed us something simply because we were from a group treated as an underclass. After all, this was America and with God on the team, the possibilities were endless.

No victim mentality from us, but awareness of how we would be perceived due to the actions of others of our race and ethnicity. Unfortunately for African Americans, perceptions have been made primarily from the negative actions of a few. No worries, we were aware and knew that our actions might help others gain opportunities if we did things honorably and right. Often, when meeting us and talking with us, people are surprised by our demeanor and attitudes. We are not angry, but a bit saddened

"Remembering the early struggles that challenged her standards, she was often tempted to compromise. 'It's easy to get drawn into a lack of integrity when you have to eat,' Brenda says with her incandescent smile and easy laugh. But her faith and determination kept her on the high road." (St. Louis Woman Magazine, March 2007 by Susan Fadem)

by the wasted lives and energy by those creating the disenfranchisement and those experiencing it.

I contend that the reason so many people who make it fast to stardom or power then "crash and burn" is because they did not develop or have time to create a firm foundation. It is important to develop a solid foundation of values, principles, skills, and a strong work ethic so that it will not crumble in good times or in challenging times. This is because no matter where you are, what you have or who you are with, you will have challenging times.

Know Where You Stand Before You Stand

I was quite surprised to discover how many people so easily slant ethics and expect others to just follow along. By fifty plus years you would think one had a strong sense of this, but I admit one event totally surprised me and demonstrated how corporations became "slanted."

After being in business over ten years with revenues exceeding $16,000,000 and the economy a challenge, we were blessed with being awarded a $5,000,000 contract. It was actually a one-year $1,000,000 contract with four option years of $1,000,000 each. We had been approached by a subcontractor to team with them as the prime contractor who had the government agency relationship. Our business developer, program manager, proposal team, and contract manager all worked diligently on the proposal to bring in the win. It was a great boost to the revenue potential and definitely needed because no contracts are forever. We had a couple of contracts that were near the end of the period of performance so this new one would be a great help to our financials.

Several weeks into the beginning of the work, it was brought to my attention that the subcontractor's time reporting was not correct. They were reporting hours and staff that had not been working on the contract. Since it was time and materials, it was critical that the reporting be documented correctly. Rather than submitting an invoice and signing it as true and correct to the best of my knowledge, I continued to send the team back to the subcontractor for correction.

After a few months the subcontractor still would not correct the time reporting and then began to complain to the contracting officer that we failed to pay them. That was true because it was our only leverage to get correct data. Rather than submitting signed invoices knowing they were fraudulent, I requested a teleconference with the contracting officer because our team was getting "grief" from the contracting officer about not paying the subcontractor.

That morning I prayed strongly for the Lord's help in resolving this situation. During the teleconference in which our business developer, contract manager, program manager, and controller participated, I explained the situation to the Government Agency Contracting Officer.

After listening to my concern about signing fraudulent invoices with incorrect time reporting, she said, "Why do you care, you would get paid anyway?"

After swallowing and breathing deeply, I responded that I did care and did not want to commit fraud. She indicated that we needed to move forward which implied we were to ignore the fraud potential and sign the invoices knowing the accompanying time reporting was not correct. I immediately offered to transition the contract to any other prime vendor they selected and would give up the contract if we would not be cited for non-performance. We had correctly been performing and properly tracking the time.

She simply said, "Okay."

For ethics, we actually walked away from a $5,000,000 contract and proceeded to transition it to another vendor! Not everyone on our team was pleased with my stance. Some understood and were relieved it was resolved without impacting our reputation. Others were critical of my stance thinking that if the Contracting Officer knew and was fine with the false reporting why couldn't I also accept that. My belief was that it was simply unethical and no amount of money was worth the risk. This was a great impact to the business because it would have represented $1,000,000 in gross revenue per year over the next five years—quite long term for a small business. However, ethics and doing what was right was and continues to be more important.

In my journey, I often faced a crossroads, a decision, and a defining moment in which I had to decide to be a victor or a victim. What will you decide?

Nuggets for Living Fully and Successfully

Once you compromise your integrity, you can never get it back!

What does maintaining your integrity mean to you?

Who do you know that maintains their integrity even in the face of temptation?

Below are some of the life values and principles given in this chapter. Check off the ones you are already using and circle the ones you may need to begin to implement in your own life.

- Tithe or give to charity.
- Invest in appreciating assets instead of do-dads.
- Live to get out of the rat race and live on investments rather than from paycheck to paycheck.
- Love my neighbor as myself and think of everyone as my neighbor.

- Work as if for God and not my bosses or those around me.
- Try to ignore and not participate in gossip.
- Learn as much as possible and remain vigilant so I am aware of opportunities.
- Support and respect your bosses as much as possible.
- Survey the boss often to ensure you are meeting or exceeding expectations.
- Observe positive role models and those that have accomplished what you admire.
- Ask and look for how others reached what you admire.
- No victim mentality.
- Determine to give your best, go the extra mile, and strive for excellence.
- Develop a solid foundation of values, principals, skills, and a strong work ethic.
- Allow your faith and determination to keep you on the high road.

"In my mind success and power are defined as being comfortable in my own skin, accepting my decisions, moving forward, and being content with each step of my life's journey." – Brenda Newberry

CONCLUSION: VICTOR OR VICTIM?

In the past few days of reflection looking at the many people coming and going in the airports, I wondered why so many seem not to have peace. Well, at least their actions and expressions were oddly downcast with a countenance of sadness. As I observed them being mean to others and having little patience with those providing services, I thought in this land of freedom and plenty, why? Is it ego, stress, lack of respect for others, lack of manners, or anger at "the world"?

Then I heard the blaring of news at various points in the airport. Listening to the various issues and stories about fair share and white privilege gave me pause. Who promised us fairness? Certainly not God. To start with, none of us were endowed or born exactly the same, not even identical twins. Everyone, absolutely everyone has a talent. Everyone, absolutely everyone has challenges. The challenges of life and the unfairness rhetoric seem to come from a vantage point of either a feeling of being a victim, envy or desire. Perhaps even guilt when it comes from those with excess material comfort. Again I must ask, why?

Does it make one better or stronger to be a victim, to be envious of another or to simply have the desire to have something you do not?

I submit to you it does not. In fact it stifles individual growth and freedom. After all being a victim or displaying anger about being a victim does not eliminate the fact that there is a lack of something that one desires. After expressing your plight, you will still be in the same place unless you take action. When there is someone or something to blame, it shuts down the ability to assume accountability, take responsibility, and be creative in an effort to resolve the situation of "lack."

Does being envious and feeling you deserve the same as others lead to obtaining those things for which you are envious? No. Does what someone else has keep you from having it as well? No. Thinking so is only the scarcity mentality so very well discussed by Steven Covey in his book, "Seven Habits of Highly Successful People." There is abundance in this world far beyond what we could ever imagine. However, only personal action will provide an opportunity to attain it. Does simple desire result in obtaining the very thing you desire? Of course not. There is no magic wand to give you the desires of your heart (Psalm 37:4).

Practically everyone in this world is a victim of something. Whether it is the family into which one was born, their race, ethnic group, hair color, hair texture, socioeconomic status or the like. However, in spite of this we are all aware of people

> **Only acceptance of what is required and action to start movement towards those desires can accomplish such goals.**

that have overcome tremendous odds to attain some form of *success* from the young woman sexually abused to the physically or mentally challenged to the young man of alcoholic parents to the physically and/or verbally abused to the girl or boy born into extreme poverty. From Oprah Winfrey to President Bill Clinton to Dr. Ben Carson to President Barak Obama to a plethora of well know people born into or encountering something over which they had little to no control. The difference is they pulled up something within themselves to forge forward without letting their victim-hood define what was possible. They had faith. They overcame their circumstances. They did not wallow in victim-hood, at least not for very long.

Therefore, it is important to ask ourselves does my lack due to being a victim feel better because I am able to blame something, someone or some group? If we would be honest with ourselves, we would admit that in spite of being able to blame someone, the lack remains and we still feel horrible.

> **Many people end up with massive displeasure or depression as they realize the time wasted concentrating on their "victim-hood" rather than taking action to resolve their "lack."**

Choices!

Perhaps that is the reason there are unhappy people in the world and the United States in particular, the land of opportunity and plenty. They feel guilty about their "bad decisions" or lack of action. The young person that dropped out of high school. The drug-addicted. The teen mother that is struggling. The high school dropout. The college drop out. The difficult and negative employee. The blended families. The divorced adulterer. The felon. The physical or sexual abuser. The alcoholic. The lazy. The slacker.

All of these actions or in-actions most often cause major life changing future challenges. The horrible and tough challenges usually tend to be the result of choice, though not always. For example, if one is raped as a teen and becomes pregnant, this not a choice. She will be a teen mother through no choice of her own. For many of us, however, it has been a matter of choice.

There were and are times that I have regretted not concentrating and making better grades in high school Spanish, especially when I found myself stationed in Spain. Other times I regret not taking piano lessons because I would love to know how to play it now. My mother wanted me to take piano lessons. I had long fingers that she felt would make it easy for me. What a wasted opportunity. There are times I regret not reading more or praying more, resting more, meditating more, and spending more time with family. It really is not too late to do all of these things. However, if I do not and find I am later lacking something desired, it will not be because there is not fairness or that I did not get my fair share or that others have more privilege, it will be because of my own choices.

Yes, I could become a victim and say I was not born Hispanic so that is why I am not fully fluent in Spanish. I could blame my parents because they could not afford a piano. I could even blame the lack of time or the "sweat shop" environment of certain companies with which I worked for not reading or praying more. While all of this is true, we all know our own decisions affect the status and the future of our "regrets." I could have studied harder, saved my allowance and bought a used keyboard, and worked at different companies. All of which would have led to different outcomes. However, I am at peace and know many things could still be accomplished even now. It is not too late as long as one is breathing and their heart is beating.

The point is that humans seem to prefer wallowing rather than taking action. Each of us can take steps right from where we are and make changes,

Nothing is perfect and life is tough, but improvement is always possible.

take actions, and create the foundations that bring peace in our lives.

There are many stories of felons that became extremely successful after serving their time. There are stories of eighty year olds that have finally completed their college degree and college dropouts that became entrepreneurs. We read of the teen mother that went on to be a wonderful mother and raised statesmen. There are so many other examples!

Success? In my mind success and power are defined as being comfortable in my own skin, accepting my decisions, moving forward, and being content with each step of my life's journey. It is being able to give to God as biblically directed, taking care of my family (emotionally and also with "adequate" food, shelter, and clothing), and being able to do much good for and to others.

Ultimately success and power can be achieved by everyone from janitors to teachers, from cashiers to policemen, from fast food workers to CEOs, from attorneys to pilots, from lawn care workers to florists, from statesmen to actors. All of these have different "status," but all can be powerful and successful in their own right.

The challenge is to accept the state you are in, make the best of it, and perform as if whatever you are doing, you are doing it for God. If you desire something different or if God is leading you or directing you towards something else, then determine to either take action or not so that you can be at peace in your own skin and with your decisions. Every decision has consequences, but time spent on envy of others is wasted. Time spent seeking your own improvements to achieve your desires and goals is best. The result will be a countenance of peace which will be noticed as others can "feel" from your demeanor that you are comfortable in your own skin.

Brenda and Daughters All Grown Up

Final Instructions

Now we ask you, brothers and sisters, to acknowledge those who work hard among you, who care for you in the Lord and who admonish you. (1 Thessalonians 5:12 NIV)

And don't just do the minimum that will get you by. Do your best. Work from the heart for your real Master, for God, confident that you'll get paid in full when you come into your inheritance. Keep in mind always that the ultimate Master you're serving is Christ. The sullen servant who does shoddy work will be held responsible. Being a follower of Jesus doesn't cover up bad work. (Colossians 3:23 MSG)

ABOUT THE AUTHOR

Brenda D. Newberry
CEO Nesher, LLC
Founder and Retired CEO & Chairman, The Newberry Group, Inc.

Mrs. Newberry founded the Newberry Group in 1996, a global IT consultancy specializing in cyber security, networking, enterprise infrastructure, and systems integration. In March 2008, the company was transitioned to an ESOP (Employee Stock Ownership Plan) and became 100 percent employee-owned at which time Mrs. Newberry became Board Chair until the transition was completed in 2010. The company has distinguished itself as a premier cyber security and information technology services firm, having received national awards including the Inc 500 (2004, 2005, 2006) and Deloitte-Touché National Technology 500 (2001, 2003, 2004, 2005, 2006). The company also received numerous regional awards including the Greater St. Louis Top 50 award (2004, 2005, 2006, 2007). Mrs. Newberry is now a sought after national speaker and writer on topics of leadership, board service, business, and life/work balance. As a result, she and her husband founded Nesher, LLC. They also founded Aquila Property Management, LLC in 2010 to manage real estate holdings.

Besides serving as CEO with Nesher LLC., Mrs. Newberry, has served on the Board of Directors of The Laclede Group, Inc. (NYSE: LG) since 2007 (Audit, Compensation, Nomination & Governance and Investment Review Committees) and from 2007 to 2015 she served on the Board of Directors of Enterprise Financial Services Corporation (NASDQ:EFSC) (Audit and Nominating & Governance Committees).

With almost $4 Billion in revenues, The Laclede Group, founded in 1857 and listed on the NYSE since 1889, is a public utility holding company that operates two business segments; Gas Utility (Laclede Gas) and Gas Marketing (Laclede Energy Resources. The Gas Utility segment includes the regulated operations of Laclede Gas and Alabama Gas Corporation (Alagasco) both engaged in the purchase, retail distribution, and sale of natural gas serving residential, commercial and industrial customers. LER is a wholly owned subsidiary engaged in the marketing of natural gas and related activities on a non-regulated basis. In 2014, The Laclede Group announced the start of its Natural Gas Fueling Solution, SPIRE with the opening of its first CNG fueling station in St. Louis.

Founded in 1988 and with over $3 Billion in assets, Enterprise Financial Services Corporation operates as the holding company for Enterprise Bank and Trust that offers banking and wealth management services to individuals and business customers located in the St. Louis, Kansas City and Phoenix markets.

Mrs. Newberry is also a Chair Emeritus of Webster University, St. Louis, Board of Trustees where she served as chair from 2011 to 2013. She also co-chaired a United Way major gift campaign from 2012 to 2014. She has also served on many other non-profit boards in various roles including board chair of St Louis Women's Forum, United Way of Greater St. Louis

(Vice Chair and Executive Committee), United Services for Children (President), Washington University School of Engineering National Council and SSM Healthcare.

Mrs. Newberry's career in information technology began in the U.S. Air Force in 1973. A six-year USAF veteran she earned an Air Force Commendation Medal and was selected from a field of over 570,000 candidates as one of twelve outstanding airmen for the year 1978 representing the U.S. Air Forces in Europe. Before starting her own company, she worked with McDonnell Douglas, (now Boeing), and MasterCard International. While with MasterCard, Mrs. Newberry advanced to Vice President and was a successful international executive responsible for the global growth of a profit and loss business unit providing image technology banking services. She also served as an adjunct professor at Washington University in St. Louis from 1987 through 2009 teaching undergraduate and graduate Operating Systems and Network Management courses.

Mrs. Newberry holds an undergrad and graduate degree in Business Management from the University of Maryland European Division and Webster University respectively as well as an Honorary Doctorate from Lindenwood University in St. Charles, Missouri.

Mrs. Newberry and her husband, Maurice, have been married since 1972 and have two married adult daughters, one granddaughter and two grandsons.

Major awards and honors received include:
- 2013 St. Louis Woman of Achievement–Civic Responsibility
- 2012 St. Louis Forum Trailblazer Award
- 2011 Small Business Administration. (SBA) Hall of Fame Inductee
- 2011 Distinguished Citizen Award–St. Louis Argus
- 2011 Woman of Distinction, Logos School
- 2009 Director & Board Magazine, Board Members to Watch

- 2009 Girl Scouts of Greater St. Louis Woman of Distinction
- 2007 Webster University School of Business Alumni of the Year
- 2007 Distinguished Entrepreneur Award (Dr. Martin Luther King, Jr. State Celebration Commission of MO)
- 2006 IT Firm of the Year Midwest Region (MED – Chicago)
- 2006 One of 25 Most Influential Business Women
- 2006 Scott AFB Chapter AFCEAN of the Year (Armed Forces Communications and Electronics Association)
- 2006 Athena Leadership Foundation Award
- Deloitte Touché Regional Technology Fast 50 (3rd in 2001, 11th in 2002, 2nd in 2003, Regional Top 50 list in 2004, 2005, 2006)
- Deloitte Touché National Technology Fast 500 (ranked 175th in 2001, 210 in 2003, 144 in 2004, 225 in 2005, 375 in 2006)
- INC 500 America's Fastest Growing Private Business (ranked 269 in 2004, 275 in 2005)
- INC 500/5000 America's Fastest Growing Private Business (ranked 4,533 in 2006)
- 2005 SBA Missouri Small Business Person of the Year
- 2005 YWCA Special Leadership Awardee
- 2005 Missouri Chamber of Commerce Industry Fast Track
- 2004 Entrepreneur of the Year – St. Louis American and RCGA
- 2004 Tri-County Entrepreneur of the Year – Technology Sector
- 2003 Professional Organization of Women Top Ten African American Woman of Distinction
- 2003 NAWBO Distinguished Woman Business Owner of the Year
- 2003 USDA OPPM Woman-Owned Business of the Year
- 2003 NMSDC Regional Supplier of the Year
- 2002 Missouri Small Business of the Year (Governor's Award)

- 2002 USDA Rural Development Woman-Owned Business of the Year
- 2002 & 2000 St. Louis Minority Business Council Minority Business Enterprise of the Year

CPSIA information can be obtained at www.ICGtesting.com
Printed in the USA
BVOW04s1855261015

424233BV00001B/56/P